Personal Library Of
RANDALL J. MEDLIN
(14 July 87)

Vol. XII of the 20th Century Sermons series

The Power of Receiving

By

Landon B. Saunders

Published By
BIBLICAL RESEARCH PRESS
774 East North 15th Street
Abilene, Texas
79601

THE POWER OF RECEIVING

By Landon B. Saunders

Copyright © 1979
Biblical Research Press

Library of Congress Catalog Card No. 79-50142
I. S. B. N. 0-89112-312-1

All rights in this book are reserved. No part of it may be reproduced in any manner without permission in writing from the publishers except brief quotations used in connection with a review in a magazine or newspaper.

To
My Parents
Robert and Beulah Saunders
Who Kept the Humor
While Keeping the Faith

PREFACE

Almost ten years ago, in the bush country of Ethiopia, I met Dr. J. D. Thomas. He asked me to do a book of sermons. I agreed.

In the meantime, I also agreed to launch Heartbeat. I found myself consumed with forming a strategy to reach secular people with the Gospel. And, the book languished . . . never far from consciousness . . . tugging away at my conscience.

Also tugging was Dr. Thomas who has in every way shown himself to possess the patience of Job and the persistence of Paul! I can never adequately express to him my appreciation for his understanding. He even still speaks to me!

The following pages were literally formed "on the run." That will be evident as you read. I only hope that somewhere in this "raw" material a word can be found here and there to encourage someone to live in joy.

Special thanks is due my staff and other volunteers who transcribed material, edited and typed . . . all with unfailing good humor. Thanks Andrea, Lisa, Eva, Kathy, Jane, Jean and Valda. And thanks to Greg Ross for his counsel and encouragement.

CONTENTS

THE CRITICAL QUESTIONS vii
    What is the Question 1
    Certainty 9
    The Answer is "Yes" 22

JESUS: THE VITAL CENTER 29
    The God Who Came Near 31
    Faith: The Unique One 45
    Life: From "Out There" 56

HIS PEOPLE: HIS PRESENCE 67
    How the Church Lives 69
    When the Church is Real 79
    The Forever People 91
    The Flame of Fire 103

THE DISCIPLE: THE CRUCIAL LINK 111
    The Cross: The Tree of Life 113
    A Fact of "Life" 123
    Freedom: Where the Spirit Is 136

THE POWER OF RECEIVING 151
    The Gift of Loneliness 153
    The ABC's of Being Human 163
    The Power of Receiving 173

THE CRITICAL QUESTIONS

WHAT IS THE QUESTION

What is a human being?

As a society, we are probably further from an answer to this question than we have ever been. As we've grown in our knowledge of the human body and the world around us, we've become less certain that what it all means. We speak with greater certainty about microbes and molecules than we do persons. We know how to get to the moon; we don't know how to direct our lives.

The Cry

A book title says: *Man Was Not Born to Cry.* Yet, from the beginning of humanity a cry has gone up. The cry has rarely been more poignant than today.

Our Music. We hear songs about "the compromises we make on our way to our horizon." And we despair how "many more messages we're going to hear."

Today's music feels the weight of our sigh, struggles with the meaning of a groan, wrestles with unfairness and fear and expresses the general frustration, despair and emptiness of our age.

Our children know all the words by heart . . .

Science. Because of scientific advancement, we are asking, when is a person dead? Also, when do we qualify to be called a person? The debate rages. The courts often are called upon to try to decide. What is life? What is human life? The question is raised again. It won't rest.

Coping. The pressures of society, the will to survive have created a new religion of self-help techniques. Seminars and books have proliferated in the last five or six years. They have become big business.

The point of this new thrust is to help people to cope with themselves. It is designed to help people "take charge of their lives." It shows "how to take control of your life." All kinds of approaches and therapies are suggested.

Thousands are trying to make sense of their lives. They don't inquire much into the meaning of life; they concentrate on techniques. Try to make it work better even if you can't understand it.

Suicide. The alarming rise in the number of suicides, particularly between the ages of 17 and 24, points to the depth of frustration with life today. Persons reach the point where going on has lost meaning. They can find no reason to live.

Preoccupation with bills. The greatest concerns of many people revolve around bill-paying and income taxes. How to survive takes precedence over every other question. Credit reigns as king. The joy of slapping the credit card on the counter all too soon gives way to the hopelessness of matching income with expenses at the end of the month. We no longer direct our financial resources; ease of credit has brought us into a new bondage.

Value change. Complicating the issue still further is the acceptance of behavior which is grounded in nothing more solid than one's present desire. The indulgence of desire is equated with the pursuit of happiness. Instant gratification is more prized than loving commitment.

Rare have been the societies that have been more blatantly boastful of wickedness. Our wickedness is not shyly done; we herald it with pride and defiance.

WHAT IS THE QUESTION

What should a person do? How should we live?

Technological dreams. Most of our nation's priorities center in technology. We have forgotten how to formulate great ideals and how to dream great dreams for humanity. The craze for the practical has cut us off from the awe of promise. We want to make it work; we don't care what it means.

We're such an enigma. Someone said, "Man is not the answer; man is the question." Who are we? We are capable of such unspeakable horror. Yet, we remain capable of unfathomable love and caring.

Carl Sandburg expressed the mystery in a whimsical way. Viewing the tall buildings in Chicago he asked, "Who built all these buildings? Who made all these skyscrapers? Who's doing all of this?" Replying to his own question he said, "Man! The little two-legged joker. Man!"

The Undefined Human

We have defined almost every question except the human one. We have defined almost every object, every tool, every machine.

Machines and persons. We accept the definition of the machines we use every day. In fact, we take it all for granted and would be surprised if the question was ever raised. We know what a dishwasher is for. We know how it works. We know what to do when something goes wrong. We have a book of instructions and we know how to call the repairman. Yet . . . the person who made and who operates the dishwasher can't answer these same questions concerning himself or herself.

We know what our car is for, how it works, what to do

when something goes wrong. But . . . we don't have the same information for our own lives. We assume this information is not available.

We assume we are greater than the machines we operate . . . yet we are willing to live with less basic information.

We made the machines, therefore, we can say what they're for, how they work, and we can provide instruction for breakdown.

Major questions. Doesn't all this raise two basic questions about persons? *One:* Who made us? *Two:* What were we made for? Aren't these sensible questions?

How can we ever define our lives without answers for these two questions? The questions themselves help clarify our problem, don't they? We are merely asking for ourselves what we assume and know about our machines. Doesn't that make sense? Shouldn't the maker of the machines bring the same knowledge to himself he brings to what he makes?

Our personal machines have a context. Intelligence has acted upon them; they don't just happen. Doesn't the maker of the machines have a context? Did he with all his genius just happen? It's time to bring some dignified thinking back into our lives. We've lived blindly too long already.

The Defined Human

Few, if any, attempts to bring a sense of context to human life have rivaled David's for quiet elegance and rare simplicity. Let's meditate upon it again:

> When I look at thy heavens, the work
> of thy fingers,
> the moon and the stars which thou
> hast established;

> what is man that thou art mindful of
> him,
> and the son of man that thou dost
> care for him?
> Yet thou hast made him little less than
> God,
> and dost crown him with glory and
> honor.
> Thou hast given him dominion over
> the works of thy hands;
> thou hast put all things under his
> feet. (Psalms 8:3-6)

The Architect and Maker. David sees Loving Intelligence behind the world. Someone's "fingers" made it. The flower, the bird, the sun and moon and stars were made.

Man and woman were "made." We were "made," "crowned" and given "dominion." We were given "glory and honor."

Furthermore, we were made in the image of the Maker. "So God created man in his own image, in the image of God he created him; male and female he created them." (Genesis 1:27)

This is hard for many to accept. Because we cannot know God in the way we examine a molecule, we refuse to accept Him. Of course, nothing we make knows us that way . . .

We demand that we be able to fathom God completely, to know enough about Him to say, "Now, I have Him. I understand Him. I've reduced Him to my comprehension." We want to bring Him within our sphere of control.

Still, we feel it's perfectly natural for the things we make never to have this knowledge about us . . .

We have erected our own stumbling block. We have

become entangled in the foolish and unrealistic and illogical web of our own pride.

I would have expected intelligence to make us. It squares with everything I've ever known about things made and their makers.

I'm thankful for the light we have on who made us and in whose image we are made. Children who, for whatever reason, are deprived of any knowledge of their parents suffer a great loss. We know who we are when we look into the face of our father...

According to David, we receive definition from the One who made us. That is reasonable. We are like our Father.

The Purpose and Sustenance. David also provides the context in which we can find our purpose. We were given "dominion over the works" of our Maker; He put "all things" under our feet.

It is difficult to pinpoint exactly who David envisions here. Some feel he points exclusively to Jesus. If he does, I feel that no violence is done when humanity is included. There is no question but that David refers to one's humanity as opposed to divinity. If Jesus is referred to here specifically, He is envisioned in His humanity. Since we share His humanity, since He was made like us, we share with Him the hopes and dreams of God. The second chapter of Hebrews affirms our oneness with Jesus.

We find our purpose in what God is and what He has created and put us over. We are stewards of His creation. Our work is centered here. Only our relationship to God Himself antedates our relationship to our work.

Our assignment as a person grows out of the will of our Designer. That, too, makes sense and squares with what we assume every day about the things we make. To find the design and meaning for your life completely separated from the One who made you is illogical and senseless. You would never know for sure whether you were doing the thing you're supposed to do. You could never know if you're being what you're supposed to be. Not knowing what was intended for you, how could you ever know whether you're realizing your purpose?

If you can accept this, it gives you a concrete reference point for your life. It provides hope that you still can find the meaning and purpose you seek. And it will flow from the very Heart of Reality.

David not only saw context for our purpose but also sustenance for our weary spirits. Our Maker "cares" for us.

We know who we are when we know Him. The person who knows God best knows himself best. The person who knows this has found the basis for the greatest love which is our most highly prized sustenance. We live on love.

The Definition "Focused"

All that is said here finds sharp focus in Jesus. The *law of Moses* had helped with that focus—but did not have the power to forgive. We cannot live an abundant life without forgiveness. Forgiveness is the greatest thing that can happen to a human being. Paul pointed out the inadequacy of the law. (Romans 2)

Conscience seeks to monitor our attempt to live a fulfilled life. It, too, is inadequate. (Romans 2:14-16; 3:21-26)

Only in *Jesus* can we find ourselves and the life we seek.

The Hebrews writer, pointing to our failure in the exercise of the "dominion" that was given us, says "we do not yet see everything subjected." (Hebrews 2:5-8) We see the chaos about us, the confusion, the bewilderment. We see our futile attempts to construct a life out of the confusion around us.

What is our hope then? If we don't see things working out as we feel they should, if we are unable to make them work out, are we left in a world bereft of meaning with our brightest hopes and dreams forever "unrealizable"?

No, we see something that is focused and clear and exciting. "But we see Jesus, who for a little while was made lower than the angels, crowned with glory and honor because of the suffering of death, so that by the grace of God he might taste death for every one." The "glory and honor" we've lost have been recovered in Jesus. And, through Him, it is ours again! We are one with Him in "origin." (2:11) He is not ashamed to call us "brethren." (2:11) He has delivered us who "through fear of death" have been confined to "lifelong bondage." (2:15)

You have a new question: who is Jesus?

I believe He is the real definition of man. He is God's answer to the question, "What is man that Thou art mindful of him?" His plan for your life is the answer to our cry, "What must I do to be saved?"

What do you believe?

CERTAINTY

We have been asking for a long time what man really is, what his problem is, what his hope is. We can understand the Hebrews writer when he tells us that not all things have been subjected to us because a lot of things in our world really do seem out of control. (Hebrews 2:8) We may not expect that everything is going to be made right today or tomorrow, or even in a hundred years, but what we're praying for is the wisdom to understand ourselves, and to understand what it is we're to do in this world where so many things are out of control. We want to understand how we're to live. We want to understand the place of Jesus in this whole question. And we need somehow to be able to disengage ourselves from all that has happened to Him at the hands of men in the last twenty centuries, so that the truth of His life may again break through in our hearts and cause us to have hope, and cause us to rejoice with unspeakable joy. There is a place that is solid, and there is a place that is secure. There is a ground that is firm. If we seek we can find it. But then, we must have the courage to stand on it.

Certainty in a Storm

Some time ago I had quite an experience. I was headed for Pittsburgh, where I was to speak, and enroute from Dallas we boarded a Boeing 707. The aircraft was full. I was sitting in the back seat of the plane. The pilot cautioned people to remain seated. It was a bit turbulent, though not too bad. Everyone had listened to the pilot's instructions and was buckled in. More than three-fourths of the meals had been served on the plane—which is a lot of meals on a 707—when all of a sudden the emergency lights flashed, and it seemed like we ran into a mountain! But we stayed intact.

It was a cold front. A fast-moving cold front. Clear air

that the radar had not picked up. The pilot was totally unaware. And for the next 20 or 30 minutes we rode through that storm. What a ride it was!

When we first hit the thing, all the meals went to the ceiling! The drinks went everywhere. And the stewardesses went everywhere. A serving cart was coming down the aisle and was about where I was when we hit one big jolt. It went up, and everything on it came down on me. I was covered with ashes and cigarette butts, and everything from the tray that could break and get on a human being!

It was the first time on an airplane I had ever felt I was getting ready for my final appointment! I really didn't believe the plane was going to make it. We were going in every direction . . . the plane was out of control . . . pilot and passengers were at the mercy of that huge metal hulk that was creaking as it was wrenched—how in the world it stayed together, I don't know! There was general panic and bedlam aboard the plane.

One of the stewardesses completely panicked. She still hadn't settled down when we finally reached the airport. She lit a cigarette just prior to landing, which of course was against regulations.

Through all of that there was a lady sitting beside me across the aisle, and judging from her appearance, she was very wealthy with several beautiful rings on her fingers and a lovely fur around her shoulders. She was terror-stricken. It seemed like what she was wearing was all she had to trust in, and it just didn't fare very well in that time of stress.

Sometimes we think about the way we would like to meet death, but we're never quite sure until we face the possibility. But I felt right—I felt right with the people on the plane, I felt right with Landon, I felt right with God. I was overwhelmed with gratitude because of that strength and that sense of security—a calm assurance that somehow was so sustaining—that was not shaken. There wasn't the panic, nor all those questions all over again—you know—about life, about identity, what I'm for. There was just something that you hope will be there when the hour arrives, and it was all there—thanks to the grace and the goodness and the love of God.

Can a person live with that kind of security? Can he find enough answers to live with the kind of security that death itself cannot touch? Is it possible to move through the earth with a dignity that is born of certainty? Without doubting that I'm going to live right? Without doubting that I'm going to die right? Without wondering if death is going to swallow me up totally, or if there could be something beyond that? Is there a way for man to live that is sure and steadfast? Is there a center of security, a center of certitude that really can be developed at the heart and core of one's life, that will be sustaining through all the various circumstances of life? Well, I feel there ought to be.

There are some things in Romans 8 that speak very pointedly to this whole scheme. After dealing with the question of assurance in Jesus Christ in the opening chapters of Romans, Paul begins to move toward one of his grand climaxes:

> What then shall we say to this? If God is for us, who can be against us? He who did not spare his own Son, but gave him up for us all, will he not also give us all things with him? Who shall bring any charge against God's elect? It is God who justifies; who is to condemn? It is Christ Jesus, who died, yes, who was raised from the dead, who is at the right hand of God, who indeed intercedes for us. Who shall separate us from the love of Christ? Shall tribulation, or distress, or persecution, or famine, or nakedness, or peril, or sword? . . . No, in all these things, we are more than conquerors through him who loved us. For I am sure that neither death, nor life, nor angels, nor principalities, nor things present, nor things to come, nor powers, nor height, nor depth, nor any thing else in all creation, will be able to separate us from the love of God in Christ Jesus our Lord. (Romans 8:31-35, 37-39)

Now, that's a thrilling passage, isn't it? Look at the possibilities here. The things that can separate us—the things that can threaten man—the things that can intimidate man— things that can rob him of feeling this assurance and certainty and confidence in life and in death—the things that will bring anxiety are listed here. Then he begins picking them off: tribulation—would tribulation shake you in your life? Remember in 1962, the day when President Kennedy appeared on television and began to talk about the crisis with Russia over the Cuban missile sites? I was in the front yard and people stopped by—people were tremendously upset. We had a rousing worship assembly the next night—people trying to get right with God. Tribulation, you see there is something about tribulation that's threatening. There was something about the possibility of war, something about bombs, something about missiles that suddenly caused people to think about themselves. But it seems so sad that a man doesn't think about himself until the hour of crisis. After all, who can think straight in the hour of crisis?

So Paul asks, can tribulation shake you up? Can tribulation rob you of your security, the ground on which you're standing? The foundation of your life—can it stand when the fires of tribulation burn? If we are made in the image of God, then we ought to be able to rise above all of these circumstances. We should be able to rise above even the elements, in absolute defiance of them! The storm waters may rush over us, and they may destroy us, but we go down with certainty! We are not the victim or the prisoner of a wave. Surely we're not that!

Or "distress." Will distress shake you? What are you trusting? In whose name are you travelling? What is it that gives the spark to your life? Persecution . . . famine . . . the loss of your job. What does it do to your life? A man on the West Coast had a good job, a good paying job. He lost his job. The next week he lost his faith.

Nakedness, peril, swords, death, life, angels, principalities, things present, things to come, powers, height, depth, anything. Do you know why these things are threatening to people? It's simple. These things are threatening to people because this is the place where they have chosen to build their lives. You see, the foundation of their lives, the name in which they are travelling is all tied up in these things. Their meaning comes from these things. Their meaning is tied up in some things that tribulation can threaten. That distress can threaten. That famine can threaten. That nakedness, peril, or sword can threaten. If the basis of my life, the meaning of my life, is vulnerable to these things, then the possibilities of my living with much certainty are pretty few. Because these are matters that we will never escape. As long as you live, you are going to wrestle with all of those possibilities. Life isn't going to be an easy street. It's not going to be a life of circumstances where everything is wonderful and just fine. It's not going to be that way. Somehow, you're going to lose a child here, or a mate over there. Or a job somewhere else. There's going to be a reverse here.

Here we are, moving along through life. Things are going just great. The wife's fine, and the children are fine. Their health is fine. And the job's fine. It's just wonderful. And everybody thinks, "I'm unshakable. There's nothing that can get to me. I'm happy, and I've really got it together." Then suddenly, one little tiny germ can work its way into the small, frail body of your daughter, and just cut you down and weaken you to the point that you can hardly gather up the strength to stand by an oxygen tent long enough to watch her die.

You say, "Now wait a minute! We were going to talk about good news!" Listen. Reality doesn't have to be bad news. And to talk about the good news we don't have to live in a "Let's pretend" world. Life is complex. Life is difficult. It is struggle. It always has been, and I guess it always will be. It isn't easy for a man to be born—to try to get that first breath. It takes all his energy to keep on breathing as long as he lives. Then one day, when it comes time for that last breath, he's not ready.

The whole point is that your certainty cannot be any greater than that to which your certainty is tied. It can't be any more secure than the ground on which your certainty rests.

There was once a rich young ruler who was intrigued by Christ. He was intrigued with this whole idea of religion, and was himself a religious person. Yet, he knew that something in his life wasn't quite right. Somehow it just didn't fit together as he knew it should. He had an uneasy feeling deep down in the quiet moments of his life like you, when the family is gone, when the television sets are all shut off, and the radios are down, when you are drinking that cup of coffee in the morning before the family has risen. You sit down. The house is still, the morning is quiet, and you find yourself beginning to ask those personal questions. The ones that aren't easy. What you're all about. You begin to wonder. And you begin to question.

This rich young ruler was in that predicament. He had so many things. He was surrounded with luxuries, but that wasn't the point. The point was that in him—in his head, in his heart, in his being—there was just a touch of uneasiness, a touch of emptiness. And given the right set of circumstances, he just didn't feel very comfortable. His collar could get tight mighty fast. He could become a little afraid, and the old specter of dread would rise up within him, and he could feel himself choke.

So he says, "Good Master, what might I do to have this eternal life, this kind of life? I recognize that the kind you are talking about is not the kind I have—even with my wealth."

Jesus says, "Keep the commandments." He begins where we're able to begin.

The young man replies, "I've kept all of those. What lack I yet?"

Jesus says, "All right. Your certainty, the meaning of your life, the basis of your life is in your possessions. As long as the basis of your life is in your possessions, you're not going to know confidence. So get rid of all of that. You sell off all that and follow me. And then you'll have it." (Matthew 19:16-22)

Why did He tell him that? Why didn't He tell everybody that? Because everybody doesn't have the same problem. This man's problem was that his life was all tied up in the things around him. And therefore, when the things around him were threatened, he was threatened.

Think over some of the past introductions you've had. Somebody approaches, and you say, "I'm John, and I'm an engineer." He's Joe, and he has the local florist shop. And here's Sue, she's a housewife. As though our identity is what we do. Now, that's important, but that's not the whole story. What's going to happen the day you get a form to fill out which says "occupation"—and you're no longer employed? Or you've been retired. Then what are we going to do? You see all those things are important facets of life, but they are not the solid kind of material—they're not the stuff out of which solid foundations for living can be made. Things which can give a man assurance and certainty and confidence for all the storms of life.

Luke describes a rich fool in the 12th chapter, who surveyed his barns and thought, "My, this is a prosperous operation that we have going here! And the barns are overflowing, and this is a land of plenty. Bumper crops every year. I've got a problem—what am I going to do?" Jesus told that story, probably with a rich man sitting there, who was thinking, "My, my, He knows my story. It's just as though He was over with me last night and had dinner at my place."

Jesus kept talking about all these barns. And this rich

man was just feeling great. Anybody who was there could be feeling great to that point. But then, Jesus dropped it on him. He said, "Tonight you'll die." All of a sudden that put the whole operation in a different perspective. Then whose things shall these be? Jesus provided brilliant insight when He said, "A man's life does not consist in the abundance of his possessions."

Now you say, "That's just so religious . . ." No, that's the truth. If you'll think about it you'll see that Jesus spoke the truth. A man's life is more than what he does. A man's life is more than what he owns. And, as long as our lives are all tied up there, every time that's threatened, whether it's by depression, whether it's by unemployment, or whatever it is, it's going to threaten me, and I'll be intimidated as a human being—a victim, a prisoner of my culture. A victim of circumstances over which I have absolutely no control. I don't want to be like that. It's unworthy of a human being. It is not the dignity that a human being deserves.

If you're living like that, listen: there is a life that you haven't touched yet. There is a life that you don't know about yet. If life is tied to these things that are subject to the stresses of life, then we're not going to know much certainty— not in an airplane, nor anywhere else.

But, there is a place to which a human being can come, that no dollar can touch. That's the important place of your life. If you could find a place to stand at that point, you could take anything. You could be human in a way that you never dreamed was possible. And I don't mean to oversimplify at all. I'm just saying the glory, the majesty, the brilliance, the dignity and the keenness of man isn't to put foundations under everything that he knows—except his own life. We've been duped. We've been deceived.

The Uncertainty Among Christians

You know, sometimes and I'll speak gently here—sometimes as Christians, we're shaken up about the wrong things. There are some words of Jesus that we don't know what to do with. When He says, "Do not be anxious about your life, what you shall eat or what you shall drink . . ." (Matthew 6:25)—that passage has a way of making us so uncomfortable. But it shouldn't. That shouldn't shake a Christian. A Christian should know what Jesus is talking about.

And Jesus says if you're slapped on one cheek, turn the other. (Matthew 5:39) You know, it's hard to figure out exactly what circumstance He was talking about there. And to be quite frank, when we get through, we conclude that there are no circumstances today that would warrant that kind of behavior.

We as Christians can become dependent on the wrong things and find ourselves puzzled, confused and threatened by Jesus' lifestyle that's so different from ours. It shouldn't! No Christian ought to be threatened by any lifestyle, if it's an honest one.

The problem is not the kind of society we're in. The problem is not the kind of clothes Jesus wore. The problem is not the kind of food Jesus ate. The problem is the attitude and view of human rights that Jesus had, that sometimes we don't share. That's what the problem is. It isn't in the circumstances that surround us. It isn't in the cultural surroundings. Jesus just didn't place His trust in many of the things we are prone to place our trust in.

I don't think that means that all Christians have to go out and sell Electras and buy Volkswagens. That's the normal reaction. "Well, what do you want me to do, preacher, sell my Cadillac?" Well, you figure that out. You have a brain. You have a heart, you have a relationship with God. I'm going to trust your judgment. If you're honest and you're open to God, if you're reading His word, and if you're trying to understand, if you're looking and if you're listening, and if you're placing it before God, you may not have any certainty where that is concerned right now, but God will help. He'll answer our prayers. We can grow into that, so we don't want to feel upset and threatened with it, but we must raise the question: *in what do you place your trust?*

Christians need to ask that. The church needs to ask that, because we've got a culture that's looking upon us and saying, "We frankly don't see enough difference in the way you live and the way we live to warrant the trouble of coming to where you are." They will see that difference, however, if we base our lives on Jesus and allow Him to transform us into His image.

Our mistake is we often place our faith in people. Our doubt and uncertainty arises when we take our eyes off the Head of the church and focus on ourselves.

For example, sometimes we look at our young people and think, "Oh my, what in the world is the church coming to." Or clearer still, "What in the world has come to the church?" And sometimes younger people will say, "What are we going to do with those elders? What are we going to do with those preachers?" If the object of your faith is people, then you have a problem. What we need is people who know in Whom they've placed their faith.

We need strength. We need courage. We need maturity. Not fear, not dread, not cowardice. We just need to stand so that nothing will shake us, nor threaten us, nor intimidate us. Let's be strong, my brother. Let the country do what it will. Let happen what will. If God is for us, who is against us? Let's live in that kind of confidence. And the church will be better.

The Uncertainty of Self

My faith doesn't rest on my ability to do right all the time. You know I can really blow it badly. A few months ago I was supposed to speak to a pretty elite group. So, I was thinking about all these little things I was going to do, because it was important. But when I got there, I just bombed out badly! I left so low. I was so ashamed, I couldn't think. Nothing went right, everything went wrong. I wanted to slip out the back door. But while I was driving through the night feeling so miserable, all of a sudden I got away from it just long enough to see that crazy performance I had just given—it was funny! There I was, driving alone, and I began to laugh. And I laughed, and laughed.

Our faith can't be in our own abilities. God loves us. He's drawing us to Himself through His precious Son. And, we need to live in that kind of assurance.

The Certainty of Jesus

Jesus' Certainty
What is the source of our faith? Jesus! But is He really the source of our faith? You say, "Well, yes." All right, what about Him? Is it the fact that He was born in Bethlehem? Or the fact that He was a great healer? Great teacher? Died a martyr's death? All that's marvelous. But it wouldn't be enough. That, at best, would just place Him among the great teachers of the earth. But you see, what the Bible says is that God did something in that Man for you and for me. God was with Him. God was in Him on the cross, reconciling us to God.

When you get to the death of Jesus Christ, was Jesus afraid? Tribulation? Yes! Distress? Yes! Persecuted? Murdered! Famine? "I thirst." Naked? Peril? A sword? It was thrust in His side.

But He won. God raised Him. If you can believe that and you can set your feet on that ground, you're unshakable. Nothing can separate you from God's love. What can hit you that didn't hit Him that day? It was like all the powers of Hell broke loose. But He absorbed it. And He was not defeated.

He said, "Lift me up from the earth and I'll draw men to me." (John 12:32) He was lifted up from the earth, and He won. He triumphed. He's the victor.

He seemed defeated, but He wasn't disillusioned. He wasn't disappointed. His disciples were. But He wasn't because He knew in whose name He was travelling. He knew the ground on which He walked. He believed in God. He trusted in God. He lived according to God's will. And He knew that the same God who walked with Him, and sustained Him, and strengthened Him, and empowered Him during those thirty-three years, was going to be with Him in the unconsciousness of His death, so that when He awakened He would be safe in the Father's hands. That was His assurance.

Certainty in Jesus
The basis of certainty is all contained in this line—"I believe that Jesus Christ is the Son of the living God." There is no more solid ground on which a man can stand. That faith means that circumstances cannot affect the meaning of your life. Nothing can shake you, or threaten you, or intimidate you. When you are anchored there, the very storm of death by execution will leave you with the strength to say as you die, "Father, forgive them for they know not what they do."

Remember this: "All things work together for good for them that love the Lord—to them that are called according to his purpose." (Romans 8:28) When you interpret that passage, don't let it get "greasy." That's a greasy passage.

For example, think about my experience on the airplane. Everything worked together for good for them that loved the Lord. But what if it had crashed? Then, what would that have done to me, according to this passage? Embarrassed me? All things work together for good to them that love the Lord —that includes God's own Son dying on the cross! All things work together for good to them that love the Lord—that means Stephen being stoned to death. All things work together for good for them that love the Lord means Paul being beaten and suffering shipwreck, and being stoned and left for dead, and being imprisoned, and probably, finally getting his head cut off on the execution block. All things work together for good to them that love the Lord means the old man John, the last apostle, banished to the isle of Patmos—exiled. He's not promising us that faith in Him removes us from the realities which all men face, which people have had to deal with since the beginning. The circumstances are still there. They don't go away. The tribulation remains. The distress remains. The persecution, the famine, the nakedness, the peril, the sword—they don't go away.

We need something that is real. Something to give us courage and stability in the midst of the storm. A certainty that allows all things to work together for good, even death—even death on a cross. A faith on which life can be built and within which life can have meaning. One that frees us from suffering and guilt and that internal pain which sometimes embarrasses us that we're even alive.

Jesus is the only One who can really give meaning to all of that. We can endure because His strength is our strength. That's the faith of a Christian. It's a real faith.

You might think, "I'd give anything in the world if I could believe that." I want to tell you that it's true. It works. It's right. And if you've been the victim of your past, the prisoner of yourself and your ego, but you're really serious about setting your life on the right track, then Jesus says, "I am the light of the world." He'll shine into your heart. Believe that He is the Christ—God's Son. You can turn from your self-rule and be identified with Him in baptism. Then, by God's power that raised Jesus from the grave, you can be raised from the grave of baptism to walk in newness of life.

It's a great invitation. Not one that we issue in our name—but in the loveliest name of all—the name of Jesus.

THE ANSWER IS "YES"

Again you have heard that it was said to the men of old, "You shall not swear falsely, but shall perform to the Lord what you have sworn." But I say to you, Do not swear at all, either by heaven, for it is the throne of God, or by the earth, for it is his footstool, or by Jerusalem, for it is the city of the great King. And do not swear by your head, for you cannot make one hair white or black. Let what you say be simply "Yes" or "No"; anything more than this comes from evil. (Matthew 5:33-37)

For the Son of God, Jesus Christ, whom we preached among you, Silvanus and Timothy and I, was not Yes and No; but in him it is always Yes. For all the promises of God find their Yes in him. That is why we utter the Amen through him, to the glory of God. (II Corinthians 1:19-20)

I remember reading an article several years ago entitled "Yes" and "No." The answers were in response to a subtitled question which read, "If you could ask but one question, what would your answer be?"

Is life's answer a Yes or No? Can we affirm life or must we deny it? Is your life Yes ... or No?

The Weakness of Contemporary Words

In our society words have lost much of their power and meaning. Language has been scrambled. Credibility pushed beyond the limits.

A few years ago the motto by which men tried to live was: Your word is your bond.

Today, that has been replaced by the warning: Let the buyer beware.

THE ANSWER IS "YES" 23

We have steadily moved from confidence in people to suspicion. Ours is an age of "bureaucrateze," which means "neutral communication." Meaning can't be attached to the words or sentences. Non-communication has become the communication.

Ours is an age of "double talk" and "buzz" words. The true feelings or beliefs of the one speaking are worded in such a way to communicate whatever the listener wants to hear. Each person hears in his own prejudices and biases and opinions wherein he was born! The speaker slips away having satisfied all!

Advertising often contributes to the confusion. Can you honestly believe what advertising promises—if not outright, then by implication? Probably nothing has done more to weaken the power of promise than advertising and politics!

What about the news? Do you believe what you hear? Do you feel you know the "real story" behind the Patty Hearst case? Watergate?

And what about the politicians? How much *do* you (not *can* you) believe?

And dare I put religion in the list of things that have weakened the power of words and promises? Religion may well be the biggest offender of all. It is long on words, oh, count the words. It would take a computer. Religion promises the sky. Then why haven't people accepted it? Why have they turned away by the millions? Can it deliver? Does it?

We are bombarded every day with words, words, words. Words, like a mighty flood, come so fast and thick they all merge into a meaningless blur. Distinction and precision are lost in the sea.

As a result, words mean very little today. We no longer trust them. And, of course, when we no longer trust words, we can no longer trust people. And when trust breaks down, chaos is never far away. A great civilization cannot be built on distrust.

What is the tragedy here? As just stated, when words can't be trusted, people can't be trusted. Therein lies the tragedy of tragedies.

Can we trust people? The little cameras and mirrors in shops and stores say No. Security measures at airports say No. Plainclothes security guards and detectives in shopping areas say No. White collar, blue collar, no collar—we assume we will be "ripped off." Check everything. Trust nothing.

How refreshing and hopeful are the words of Jesus in such a situation: "Let what you say be simply 'Yes' or 'No'; anything more than this comes from evil."

The Power of the Disciple's Yes

Jesus tells us something about the *power* of His disciple's words. When one of His followers says Yes, you can tie to it.

Oaths Do Not Strengthen the Disciple's Yes
When a disciple says Yes or No, you can do nothing to make it stronger. Nothing you add will give it greater force. Not oaths. Adding heaven, earth, Jerusalem or your own head will not strengthen the disciple's simple Yes or No.

We have learned to beware of the person who always feels compelled to prove what he's said by another person (his wife, for example). If you tell the truth, no further guarantee is needed.

Nothing is Stronger Than Truth
If it is truth, you can't strengthen it. If it isn't, nothing you add will change the falseness of it. What is the strongest

thing in the world? A disciple of Jesus' simple Yes or No. Nothing is stronger than a person who speaks truth.

Revolutionary Implications
So what does this say to a society? I'm convinced this has revolutionary implications for our society. *Consider labor, for example.* Isn't one of the greatest problems of labor the inability of employers to find employees they can trust? Whether it's lying about sickness; stealing time through habitual lateness, stretched noon hours and coffee breaks; sneaking out supplies; falsifying expense accounts. Words mean almost nothing.

Our labor problems—spiraling costs, inflation, unemployment—how many of them could be cured by a return to simple honesty? Will the kingdom of God break into these conditions?

And what about marriage? Doesn't the high divorce rate reflect the untrustworthiness of the Yes spoken at the vow exchange? Why do we go on lying at the time of the marriage vow? Why don't we say, "Maybe I will." Or, "Perhaps." Or, "It all depends on whether you wrinkle or not." Or, "Unless another person enters, stage left, who 'understands' me better."

The problem of marriage is finding a person who knows how to say Yes. And who can make it stick.

Nothing is so powerful as two disciples who know how to say Yes looking into each other's eyes and promising never to forsake each other . . .

And child-rearing? This gives new insight to child rearing. What, basically, are we trying to teach the child? Are we not trying to rear our sons and daughters to say Yes and No? If you succeed in teaching your child to say Yes, haven't you reared the strongest person imaginable? What strength of character! How trustworthy!

Do your children know how to say Yes and No?

When your children are out of your sight, when they one day leave your home, this will be crucial. Will they know how to say Yes and No? Can they trust themselves? Can you trust them? Can others?

What about our commitment to Jesus? You and I said, "Yes, I'll follow you." Can He trust your Yes? Will you stand? When you're discouraged, will your Yes hold? When you've been hurt and disappointed? When someone wrongs you? When doubt tightens itself about your heart, will your Yes hold?

And your commitment to each other? "By this we know love, that he laid down his life for us; and we ought to lay down our lives for the brethren." (I John 3:16) Jesus backed His Yes to you and me with His very life; will you back your Yes to Jesus and to your brothers and sisters with your life?

If you back it by giving your life, it's total. That's true because it's the only way you can give your life—all or none. Nobody half dies! If you lay your life down, you do not take it back when someone offends you, hurts you, talks about you, irritates you, disappoints you.

Isn't this powerful? Can you think of more *powerful relationships?* These are *relationships* you can trust. Whether in work, marriage, your children, your walk with Jesus or your walk with each other.

And here we see the real strength of the body of Christ. It is strong because its *relationships* are strong. The "gates of hell" are powerless against such a fellowship. Jesus has backed His Yes to us with His life; we back our Yes to Him with our lives; we back our Yes to each other with our lives. This is power!

The Answer to Suffering: Yes

"In him it is always Yes."

Jesus, Lord of heaven and earth, who is and always will be, is life's Yes.

Natural Disasters
Tornadoes, floods and earthquakes—they destroy thousands every year. Is their word final? No, Jesus spoke to the winds and waves and they obeyed Him. (Mark 4:35-41) One lives whose word is mightier than the natural elements. When the storm is over, Jesus is there . . .

Sickness and Disease
He opened the eyes of the blind man. "What's the answer, sir?" With lips trembling with excitement and joy he says, "Yes." Blindness does not have the last word; Jesus does. And so He looks forth into the future and says to the blind of all ages, "Remember, there is a power in the universe greater than your blindness."

He opened the ears of the deaf. He unlocked the tongues of the mute. He strenthened the legs of the paralyzed. Cleansed the skin of the leper.

Did He cure all who were diseased? No, He cured enough for the world to know that disease is not final. Its power and hold over you are not permanent. There's One whose word is stronger. When the final history has been written, sickness, suffering and disease will not have emerged the winner; Jesus is the Victor. His word is final.

And Guilt?
Is guilt final? Not in the presence of Jesus. The adulterous woman was caught in the act. Men condemned her. Jesus saw promise in her. "Neither do I condemn you; go, and do not sin again." (John 8:1-11)

Jesus' word of forgiveness is greater than the load of our guilt. No matter how great your guilt, Jesus is greater. Like the waves that became still at His word, so your troubled heart will become quiet when His word of forgiveness reaches you.

And Death?
Even death is not final. Lazarus was called forth from the tomb. "Lazarus, what's the answer?"

"The answer is Yes." (John 11)

Jesus took death upon Himself. As God's Son He wrestled with it and won.

> Since therefore the children share in flesh and blood, he himself partook of the same nature, that through death he might destroy him who has the power of death, that is, the devil, and deliver all those who through fear of death were subject to lifelong bondage. (Hebrews 2:14, 15)

"Fear not, I am the first and the last, and the living one; I died, and behold I am alive for evermore, and I have the keys of Death and Hades." (Revelation 1:18)

Jesus lives! The answer is Yes.

One must decide at some point whether we journey toward life or toward death. We must decide whether *life* will have the final word, or death. We must decide whether suffering is the answer, or resurrection.

For those who trust Jesus, God's love is greater than anything that happens to us.

> For I am sure that neither death, nor life, nor angels, nor principalities, nor things present, nor things to come, nor powers, nor height, nor depth, nor anything else in all creation, will be able to separate us from the love of God in Christ Jesus our Lord. (Romans 8:38-39)

The answer *is* . . . Yes!

JESUS: THE VITAL CENTER

THE GOD WHO CAME NEAR

To know God is to know who we are.

The one who knows most about God knows most about mankind.

In God we find what is real. Our struggles with illusion—in our lives, in our worship and in our homes—grow out of our confused thinking about God.

For some reason, we assume we cannot really know God, so we've given up trying. Solid knowledge about God isn't possible so why bother, we say. And since *nobody* knows, we think our chances with the unknown will be as good as the next person's.

I'm amazed at how quickly we conclude that we cannot know God. Most reach the conclusion with little or no effort at all. In fact, most decide on the basis of what someone else has said. And, chances are, that person decided on the basis of what still another said. Often, when you reach the end of the string of persons, either no one had taken the time to think it through or some person was embittered by a very bad religious experience.

Most unbelief rests on the flimsiest of knowledge—the least amount of thinking and research. Millions of people have been perfectly willing to entrust their very lives to such shabby thought! I find that hard to understand.

As thinking persons, we are called upon to think this matter through. The answer may be nearer than we think.

One God, One Commitment

Paul wrote, there is "one God and Father of us all, who

is above all and through all and in all." (Ephesians 4:6) What an absolutely remarkable statement. One God who is Father. Interesting. One God who is *above, through* and—what's even more absorbing—*in* all. A God who is near.

To the Corinthians he wrote:

> For although there may be so-called gods in heaven or on earth—as indeed there are many "gods" and many "lords" —yet for us there is one God, the Father, from whom are all things and for whom we exist, and one Lord, Jesus Christ, through whom are all things and through whom we exist. (I Corinthians 8:5,6)

We exist *for* Him and *through* His Son, Jesus. No statement ever uttered touches our nature so profoundly. Our being is intricately bound with His. Not only is the *reason* for our existence given here (we exist *for* Him) but also the *means* by which the reason is carried out (we exist *through* Jesus).

If you can accept this truth, do you see the deep implication it has for your life? Can you see why you haven't been able to make sense out of your life up to now? Do you see what's been missing?

Jesus was once asked what was the great commandment. His answer strikes deeply into the nature of human existence. He said,

> The Lord our God, the Lord is one; and you shall love the Lord your God with all your heart, and with all your soul, and with all your mind, and with all your strength. (Mark 12:29, 30)

Jesus envisions the whole of man concentrated into God. A person is to love God with all the heart, soul, mind and strength. Nothing about us is left over. Heart, soul, mind and strength—what else is there?

A Centering For Life

We are told to center our lives, to concentrate them, to focus them on one thing. Such concentration implies power. We are weak as persons because we are so scattered, so torn, divided among so many things. If only we could gather our lives up and concentrate them on something central . . .

You shall love God with everything you have. How different from those who declare, "Life is terrible." Or the young lady who wrote me saying, "I don't know why I should go on living."

A lot of people don't know why they should go on living. They don't know why they get up in the morning. They don't know what the end of their life is going to be. We're aimless creatures. We've lost our mooring, our sense of direction. We're "wandering stars." We hardly know where we've been, much less where we're going. We're just kind of drifting along.

Do you say thinking about these matters is pointless and discouraging? Do you realize that one of the sorriest things that ever happened to the human race was the suggestion that you can either take or leave matters such as this? You can't take it or leave it. It's not that kind of question. This question strikes at the very root of your life. It could *be* your life!

One of the most promising things I can tell you is, you *can* think this through. You can find an answer.

A World View

Psychologists tell us that people who are mentally ill somehow put the world together wrong. Thus, their entire point of view is jaundiced, and their behavior violates relationships.

What is your view of the world? Do you know how you've put it together? You've constructed some kind of view—you can count on that. It may be blurred, but you have your way of dealing with the realities of the world—even if it's to ignore them!

Often young people go off to college with a world view that includes faith in God. Then they meet some professor who asks questions they can't answer. They feel intimidated, but they never pause to think that they are being asked to answer in a few minutes what some professor has debated for years. They are not prepared either in thinking or experience to cope with such confrontations. So they "lose their faith."

The same thing has happened to a lot of older people in a different way. They are working and living and going through all the motions of life only to realize one day that they don't know why. They don't know what they believe. If you questioned them about their faith, they would be elusive and unsure.

Much of our faith is like a patchwork quilt. As we were growing up we learned a few incidents from the Old Testament. Creation. Moses leading the children out of Egyptian bondage. The call of Abraham and sacrifice of Isaac. The temple.

From the New Testament we learned about Jesus' birth and baptism. Perhaps a parable here and there, a few miracles, His death and resurrection. A piece here and there, but it never really all came together enough to make sense in our day to day lives. So many are left forever to face the world with a fractured point of view and a disjointed biblical concept.

A Place To Stand

How different we might feel if we saw how all the parts fit together—if we could see the symmetry and harmony of things. We could then see the meaning of singing birds and fragrant flowers and beautiful grass and people. We could make sense out of both the good and evil in people. We could acknowledge justice, decency and mercy, but we would also be able to reckon with the injustice and cruelty. We would have found the common theme that sets everything in its right perspective.

With such a perspective we would have a solid place to stand. We could face anything the world flings at us. Come disease. Come evil. Come illness. Come financial reverses. Come famine. Come flood. Disaster. Conspiracy. War. Come the death of a child. Bring in life's best, bring in life's worst— we can stand, we can take it.

Do you have such a place to stand?

Or, is your ground shaky? Do you have to tread lightly because your life is precariously balanced on a thin edge? You are fragile. You've simply had to close the doors on a lot of things you couldn't bear to face. Hence, every day you must be careful lest you upset your balance and be thrown into depression, confusion and even despair. You have no strength.

A Target

Having a place to stand allows you to focus on the target of your life. You can ask with greater dignity and fearlessness, "What is the goal of my life?" Do you know what your goal is? How can you know whether you're winning or losing if you don't know where the goal line is?

That's not a crazy question. It's not a moot point. It's a real question with a real answer. The ant knows its formula. So do the birds and the fish. They know what they're to do and they go about doing it.

Doesn't man have a formula?

We've allowed ourselves to drift. We've been narcotized. Our finest sensitivities have been dulled. We get up in the morning, and we plod through the day, and we hopefully sleep that night, and then we get up the next morning and do the same thing over again for a few years till we die, and some words are spoken over us and we're put in the ground. If our faces told the real story their last expression would be one of puzzlement and confusion over what it was all about. No point of view.

You do not have to live that way.

And as long as I'm alive I refuse to live that way.

Where do we start to get life on course? Let's start with some preliminary thinking about God. We'll look at some of the problems. Some of the objections.

Thinking About God

"I'm not able to raise the big questions." But you are! You don't have to live a dull life and die like a dog. You're aware. Conscious. You have dignity. Take off your coat and wade into these matters. Don't be afraid. We'll move through gently and steadily—together. You are not alone in your quest.

"I'm afraid to risk my present beliefs." But if they're shaky, you need to know it now as we examine those beliefs together. We'll always be putting something strong in the place of what's being discarded. You'd trade shaky ground for solid ground. You'll be able to enjoy the rest of your life in a way you never dreamed could be so solid and real. You'll experience a freedom you didn't even know was possible but always wanted.

We must be on guard for a closed mind. As one faces the question of God with all His power and majesty and mercy and love, we may decide we like our ignorance better! Or as you feel certain present beliefs questioned, you may feel threatened, angry. You may want to close the door tighter than ever. Be on guard for such feelings and reject them at once. Your faith must not be so fragile. If your faith is too fragile to face the questions, it is certainly too fragile to live by.

"What difference does it make what a person believes?" This question separates living from believing. It contends that living is the primary thing; therefore, isn't it more important to get on with living instead of believing?

Now, really, isn't that a bit shallow?

What your son believes about morals will make a lot of difference in the way he treats another parents' daughter who sits next to him. What a person believes about right and wrong has a lot to say about white collar crime, the trustworthiness of employees and the safety of our streets. What a person believes determines his concept of justice, his sense of decency. What one believes determines the value he places on a human life.

Life is backed by belief.

A man lives as he believes.

If belief is wrong, life is wrong. Your goal is wrong. And this is where so many are today without anything central in their lives, anything to really give themselves to. A vacuum has moved in that leaves the multitudes running off in different directions—without national or personal goals.

"But I'm an agnostic. I don't know if God exists, and I don't think anyone else does." Think about that statement. You don't know and therefore no one else knows. You're wrong.

I know God exists.

How can you speak for me? Would you say anyone who believes this is foolish, unlearned, ignorant? Have you even honestly investigated the questions? Isn't it possible you're agnostic simply because you've never really investigated?

How can you be so sure for others? Can you speak for Abraham and Moses and David? How can you speak for Jesus and Paul? How can you speak for me? You may not know, but others do know.

"But how can a person figure out this God? There are so many hypocrites who claim to believe in Him. The whole thing just turns me off." I agree there are hypocrites. I'm sorry. I see them too, but I still believe. Hiding behind hypocrites is a little ostrich-like, if you stop and think about it. Hypocrites exist in every human endeavor. Mature people must recognize this and go on.

After all, what do you propose to do with them anyway? I've chosen to love and teach them. Would it do any good to shoot them?

I don't give up eating because of a bad cook.

Think through these cliches! Don't be ensnared by them.

"But how can you reconcile your God with all the evil and suffering in the world?" A Christian isn't blind to this dilemma. He's thought about it and has decided that faith in God and suffering in the world are not incompatible.

First, neither belief nor unbelief changes the fact of human suffering. If the entire world chose not to believe, suffering would not be reduced. The choice, therefore, is not between suffering and not suffering; the choice is the *meaning* one assigns to suffering.

Second, the Christian believes that God has joined us in our suffering—instead of remaining aloof.

For it was fitting that he, for whom and by whom all things exist, in bringing many sons to glory, should make the pioneer of their salvation perfect through suffering . . . Since therefore the children share in flesh and blood, he himself likewise partook of the same nature, that through death he might destroy him who has the power of death, that is, the devil, and deliver all those who through fear of death were subject to lifelong bondage. (Hebrews 2:10, 14, 15)

Jesus suffered and overcame. We suffer with Him and therefore share with Him the victory. The question comes down to whether suffering has the final word or whether God has the final word. If the latter, this is enormous occasion for hope and joy.

The Christian's answer to human suffering is, therefore: one, God suffered with us; two, resurrection.

"Okay, if I should decide to believe, which God would I believe in? The Africans have gods. The East has gods. How do I go about deciding?"

There are two basic approaches to finding God. One is by discovery.

I was talking to a young man recently who was trying to discover God in himself. The path of discovery causes us to look within ourselves, to look at the human situation and try to discover what God is like on the basis of what we see. Eastern religions generally follow the path of discovery. It's moving from where we are upward.

The other approach is *revelation.* What if God has revealed Himself to us? What if certain knowledge about God has been revealed? Not *exhaustive* knowledge but *adequate?*

That is what Christianity is: It is revealed religion. God has taken the initiative and has moved toward us. Supernatural presence and power have penetrated our sphere. Ours is a revealed God, not a discovered one.

The God of Revelation

The God of revelation bears a nearness to the world. He is not aloof and disinterested. His footprints are there in history.

He Created the Heavens and the Earth
"In the beginning God created the heavens and the earth." (Genesis 1:1) That is a revealed fact. God created our world.

Creation has a purpose, a destiny. That means you and I have a purpose and destiny. It is not true that everything in the world—except man—has a direction. Man is the highest point of creation! His biggest problem is his refusal to think and know what his true goal is.

He Moves in History
God didn't create and retire. His footprints are in history. He moves in the interest of what He has created. That is why He makes a difference in the way we look at the world. That is why He makes a difference in our lives. He gave us the promise that "in everything God works for good with those who love Him." (Romans 8:28)

He told us His Name. Moses, in Exodus 3, asked God what His name was. God had revealed to Moses His mission for Israel. Moses had a major part in that plan. He was to lead. Upon hearing this, Moses asked God His name. God's reply was, "I AM WHO I AM." This name suggests God's action in human affairs more than it does His eternity.

God is real and in place. "Tell your people, Moses, that I'm at home. That I am source, guide and goal of all things." (Romans 11:36 NEB)

He told us what He does. What does God do? He liberates. God frees people.

As Israel escaped from Egypt they faced the Red Sea. God delivered them safely.

God lives to free men and women. Think of that. One of God's central aims is to set you free. How different from the image of the angry God dangling us over a fiery, snake-filled pit.

The God we serve is a God who is working for us. A God of promise. A God who is patient and long suffering, who yearns for us to be happy. A God who has acted on our behalf to free us from the bondage of sin and death. He really wants us to live!

Did you know that about God?

He gave us a guide. From Sinai, God gave mankind a law. Have you ever wondered where your feelings of right and wrong came from? Have you wondered about your sense of *oughtness?* Could it arise out of your very nature, a nature that came directly from God? If we are made in God's image, then God surely knows how to make us function correctly. That is why He gave the law.

The Ten Commandments are like retro-rockets which keep us moving toward our true target. Killing gets man off track. So does lying and stealing and adultery. The commandments helped men and women see more clearly where human happiness is really found. Have you ever viewed the commandments that way? Not designed to hurt you—but to guide you to happiness.

Revealed law puts something solid at the center of human behavior. It provides some sure knowledge about acceptable and unacceptable behavior. It frees us from having to experiment totally. Someone who loves us has revealed guidelines to us. He has given us a manual of instructions that tells us about ourselves and how to make ourselves work right. Cars, washing machines and gadgets have that. Isn't it reasonable that man should have one also?

God places Himself at the very center of human life. He is the basis for meaning, for morals, for hope. He is the central force, the very spirit of creation and life.

God Came Near as a Person

Why can't such a God reveal Himself more clearly, we ask? Why can't He come near to where we are?

He did.

That is the whole mystery, meaning and power of the incarnation of Jesus.

God has been here in person.

If that fact is true, then all of life will be forever different. Your life could never be the same. The future of the world could never be the same. If God has been here in person, a new light falls on us all. How could we ever live indifferent to that fact? How could we resist even thinking about it? If God became a person, the meaning of your personhood and mine has a new meaning, doesn't it?

"And the Word became flesh and dwelt among us, full of grace and truth; we have beheld his glory . . ." (John 1:14) Jesus said, "He who has seen Me has seen the Father." (John 14:9) "This is my beloved Son, with whom I am well pleased." (Matthew 3:17)

These words cause a hush to fall upon all.

What this means is when you want to know what God is like, you look at Jesus. How near He has come!

Do you want to know how God feels about those on the

fringes of society? Look at Jesus' involvement with them. Do you want to know what God thinks about disease? Watch Jesus deal with disease. Do you want to know how God treats people who are very sinful and guilty? Look at the way Jesus dealt with the adulterous woman. (John 8:1-11) How does He regard fear? What does He think about death? Just look at the way Jesus responded to it when His friend, Lazarus, died, and you'll know. (John 11:1-44) Jesus wept. He was angry. He cried, "Come forth!" That's how God feels about death.

What is God like? Look at Jesus. See how He loved. Watch Him lay down His life for people. Here we find out how much God cares, how deeply He's willing to be involved with us, just how close He is willing to come.

And what was our response when God came near? We tried to run Him off!

Suppose we had read the plays of a certain playwright. We had seen the evidence of his work. Then one day he appears on the stage and people start pelting him with rocks and run him off.

That's what happened to God in Jesus Christ.

And still . . . He loves us.

In an assembly of scholars one day a young man arose and addressed this question to one of the most learned scholars present: "Sir, you have lived many years and have studied much. Of all you've learned, what is the most profound thing you've ever found?" The old man rose slowly to his feet, faced the young inquirer and said, "Jesus loves me, this I know, for the Bible tells me so."

He is right. In Jesus, God has come very near. We can examine Him, and understand His identity. More than that, we can base our own identity on His love.

Would you be willing to look again at the question of God's identity? Open your mind once more to the question. Reject all pressures to the contrary. Don't be afraid. Your *life* depends on it.

FAITH: THE UNIQUE ONE

Does the Christian faith take its place alongside other faiths available on today's market? Or is it unique?

Is Jesus merely one of many saviours? Did He simply embody a "Messianic nature" that had shown itself in other men, or was He the Messiah in its unique sense?

Is the Bible to Christians what the Koran is to Moslems? Or is it a unique volume?

What is the "one faith" of which Paul speaks in Ephesians 4:5? Jude referred to "the faith which was once for all delivered to the saints." (Jude 3) Paul wrote: "But what does it say? The word is near you, on your lips and in your heart (that is, the word of faith which we preach)." (Romans 10:8) Paul was known as the one "who once persecuted us" but who "is now preaching the faith he once tried to destroy." (Galatians 1:23)

Is this a faith that applies to all humankind and to which all are accountable? Or does it apply to the West only?

These questions cry out for answers today. The sharp rise of interest in Eastern religions combined with new theological approaches and definitions have presented the need once again to think precisely, clearly and biblically about these issues. We cannot assume that everyone knows the answers. Nor can we assume that any Christian can respond intelligently to these matters. Each generation, for itself, must go to the well for fresh water.

The Person of Our Faith

To begin, let's examine the *person* of our faith. "The

faith" and all that is *Christian* sprang from the presence and person of Jesus. If He should prove non-existent or mythical or just a brilliant prophet, then the whole of Christianity comes crashing down. Everything hinges on Him.

A tantalizing question constantly arose around Jesus. It was asked by family, friends, disciples, multitudes and enemies. The question—*who is He?* That question has not been asked so profoundly and persistently about any other person. There was something so compelling, so convincing, so irresistible about Him that one couldn't help asking who He was.

You looked into His eyes and it seemed you were looking into the mirror of your soul. You could see your failures, your weaknesses, yet, at the same time you could see a personal value greater than any you'd ever known. Something in Him called you out of yourself; it was moral in its tone but altogether appealing and attractive; it surfaced for you the highest and noblest and most worthwhile feeling ever experienced.

He was so strong and courageous. So certain of Himself. So calm and gentle. So commanding.

And yet, He was so approachable. The most frightened, the weakest, the poorest, the most outcast somehow felt free to walk right up to Him and say, "Hello."

Who is He?

Jesus Himself raised the question. "Who do men say that the Son of man is?" (Matthew 16:13-15) The answers were interesting. Some thought He was John the Baptist, some Elijah, others Jeremiah or one of the prophets. The fact that He was identified with these gives us insight into the kind of man He was. It compels us to find out all we can about John, Elijah, and Jeremiah and the prophets.

FAITH: THE UNIQUE ONE

Then Jesus put the question squarely to them: "But who do you say that I am?" As if to say, "All right, you've walked with me, you've heard me, you've seen me—now tell me, who do you say that I am?" Then it happened. For the first time one lone soul—on a dusty Middle Eastern trail—looked into the eyes of Another and dared to say, "You are the Christ, the Son of the living God."

Who is He?

The Christ, the Son of God.

Of Him Paul wrote:

> Who though he was in the form of God, did not count equality with God a thing to be grasped, but emptied himself, taking the form of a servant, being born in the likeness of men. And being found in human form, he humbled himself, and became obedient unto death, even death on a cross. (Philippians 2:6-8)

Dare we look? God, taking the likeness of man, a servant no less, and becoming obedient to death on a cross. What kind of God is this? Why did He do this? We whisper the words: "For God so loved the world that He gave His only Son, that whoever believes in Him should not perish but have eternal life." (John 3:16)

But Paul continues: "Wherefore God has highly exalted him and bestowed on him the name which is above every name." (Philippians 2:9) His name stands beside no other. His name is truly "Son of God." The "name he has obtained is more excellent" than those of angels. (Hebrews 1:4)

Because of who He is, "at the name of Jesus every knee should bow, in heaven and on earth and under the earth, and every tongue confess that Jesus Christ is Lord, to the glory of God the Father." (Philippians 2:10, 11) The knees of the haughty and proud, the genius, the scientist and engineer, the knees of housewives and youth, of beggars and executives —every knee will bow and confess Him as Lord.

> He is the image of the invisible God, the first-born of all creation; for in him all things were created, in heaven and on earth, visible and invisible, whether thrones or dominions or principalities or authorities—all things were created through him and for him. He is the head of the body, the church; he is the beginning, the first-born from the dead, that in everything he might be pre-eminent. For in him all the fulness of God was pleased to dwell, and through him to reconcile to himself all things, whether on earth or in heaven, making peace by the blood of his cross. (Colossians 1:15-20)

The Heart of Our Faith

What is the heart and soul of our faith, the irreducible minimum of the Gospel?

To the Corinthians it was expressed this way:

> Now I would remind you brethren, in what terms I preached to you the gospel, which you received, in which you stand, by which you are saved, if you hold it fast—unless you believe in vain. For I delivered to you as of first importance what I also received, that Christ died for our sins in accordance with the scriptures, that he was raised on the third day in accordance with the scriptures, and that he appeared to Cephas, then to the twelve. (I Corinthians 15:1-4)

This is primary to our faith. Jesus died for our sins, was buried and raised.

He died for our sins. Is that an archaic notion that has lost its relevance for human life? The answer, of course, depends on our understanding of the word *sin*.

The root meaning of this word is "to miss the mark." The archer was said to have "sinned" when he shot his arrow at the target—and missed. The word later described a human life that missed its target. It describes a life that is without aim and meaning.

The meaning of Jesus' death is that God loved us and put His life down for us. He came to meet us in our emptiness, our aimlessness. He brought meaning to the place where there was no meaning. He came to the depths of our greatest needs. He brought His life to the place of our death. He became the "pioneer of suffering" who blazed the trail out of death and despair to life and hope and opened the way to victory for every sufferer. That is why He associated Himself with the downtrodden, the guilty, the sinful—He was leading them out. That is why He suffered the shame and death of the cross—He was plunging into the depths so He could lift us up.

What is the authority on which this thought stands? It stands on the authority of God Himself. Such a rescue is God's alone. Such forgiveness is possible only at His initiative.

When God, the creator of heaven and earth, forgives you, you are certain of forgiveness. When God forgives you, you can leave your guilt. You can walk away from your fear. Your tears can become soft and gentle again. You come to life!

I am basing these expressions of confidence on the reliability of revelation. Though you may not accept the revelation you can see that if believed, it is the greatest news ever announced.

Each one of us desperately yearns to be free. That is what this Gospel is all about. Freedom. Why then, do people continue to say this Gospel has no relevance, no meaning? The Gospel, when understood, speaks more directly to the real struggle of human beings than anything else. It offers love, forgiveness, freedom and a mission that gets you out of bed in joy every morning! Now that's relevant!

God Was in Jesus

Paul states this faith more definitively in his letter to the Corinthians. He says,

> All this is from God, who through Christ reconciled us to himself and gave us the ministry of reconciliation; that is, God was in Christ reconciling the world to himself, not counting their trespasses against them, and entrusting to us the message of reconciliation. So we are ambassadors for Christ, God making his appeal through us. We beseech you on behalf of Christ, be reconciled to God. For our sake he made him to be sin who knew no sin, so that in him we might become the righteousness of God. (II Corinthians 5:18-21)

Again we ask, what was unique about Jesus? Was it His miracles? No, others performed miracles. Was it special inspiration? Others were inspired. Was it His death? Others had died—even in others' stead. Was it His resurrection? Others had been raised. While each of these are integral to His unique majesty the central truth is: *God was in Christ.* "God was in Christ reconciling the world to himself, not counting their trespasses against them." "God made him to be sin who knew no sin, so that in him we might become the righteousness of God." Here is uniqueness! Of all those who had ever lived, God was in Christ in a way unlike His presence in any other. Jesus was His Son. He was doing a work for man in Jesus. The very heart of the Gospel demands that we acknowledge this central truth. We must confess that "Jesus is the Christ, the Son of the living God."

This is to confess that He was unique in His birth; unique in His mission; and unique in His death, burial and resurrection because of *who* He was and *what* God was doing in Him.

Lest we miss the force of this confession, John speaks pointedly:

> Beloved, do not believe every spirit, but test the spirits to

see whether they are of God; for many false prophets have gone out into the world. By this you know the Spirit of God: every spirit which confesses that Jesus Christ has come in the flesh is of God, and every spirit which does not confess Jesus is not of God. This is the spirit of antichrist, of which you heard that it was coming, and now it is in the world already. (I John 4:1-3)

John says we must confess "that Jesus Christ has come in the flesh." The Christ, the Messiah, has come in the flesh. Certain facts are clear: 1) This Jesus was the promised Messiah. 2) He "has come." The language here suggests prior existence. He existed before. The One who existed before "has come" here. His identity was not conferred on Him at some point in His life here. He was not a man who excelled and so came to special consciousness. He was who He was before He came. 3) He came *"in the flesh."* Not "into" the flesh, but "in" the flesh. Jesus was not a mere man who became special after a Messianic nature entered Him. *Jesus Christ,* not simply Jesus, but *Jesus Christ* came *in* the flesh. His was not a special arrangement with God but rather a permanent union with God. Of one who makes this confession, John says, "God abides in him, and he in God." (I John 4:15)

The Faith Preached

Now we are able to detect the power of the message first spoken by the apostles, as recorded in *Acts.* One "needle-sharp" point emerged repeatedly. The preaching labored to establish the one central truth upon which all faith rests. Peter and the apostles began,

> *Jesus of Nazareth,* a *man* attested to you by God with mighty works and wonders and signs which God did through him in your midst, as you yourselves know—*this Jesus,* delivered up according to the definite plan and foreknowledge of God, you crucified and killed by the hands of lawless men. (Acts 2:22-23)

No mistake about it. Jesus was historical: "Of Nazareth." It was "this Jesus," this historical person who was acting "according to the definite plan and foreknowledge of God." "But God raised him up, having loosed the pangs of death, *because it was not possible* for him to be held by it." Jesus' resurrection was inevitable because of who He was. "This Jesus God raised up, and of that we all are witnesses . . . Let all the house of Israel therefore know assuredly that God has made him both Lord and Christ, *this* Jesus whom you crucified." On the basis of this fact and through His name the "forgiveness of your sins" was offered.

It was critical that the people be convinced that God had done something unique in Jesus Christ, and that in *this* Jesus, this single historical life, we can have the forgiveness of our sins.

In Acts 3 the emphasis is again on this single point. In Acts 4, following a healing, Peter said,

> Be it known to you all, and to all the people of Israel, that by the name of Jesus Christ of Nazareth, whom you crucified, whom God raised from the dead, by him this man is standing before you well. This is the stone which was rejected by you builders, but which has become the head of the corner. And there is salvation in no one else, for there is no other name under heaven given among men by which we must be saved. (Acts 4:10-12)

Once again, this truth is proclaimed.

One can be a Christian only if he confesses this truth without equivocation or reservation. It is an exclusive, unique ultimate confession of truth.

That is why the Christian faith cannot be shared with any other faith under heaven.

That is why Jesus is not a Saviour among several.

No other ranks beside Him.

That is why the Bible stands alone as God's revelation to man.

That is why one cannot, therefore, mix Christianity with other world religions. To put it bluntly, you cannot be a Christian *and* something else. The whole dynamic of being a Christian, as set forth in the Bible, is that one follows Christ and *no other*. While one can be a Hindu and espouse Buddhism—because the authoritative writings of Hinduism do not forbid this—to be a Christian is to follow Christ *and Christ alone*. It is to recognize that Christ has "all authority in heaven and on earth" (Matthew 28:18); to acknowledge "there is salvation in no one else, for there is no other name under heaven given among men by which we must be saved" (Acts 4:12); to confess "there is one God, the Father ... and one Lord, Jesus Christ." (I Corinthians 8:6)

Thus, one cannot be intellectually honest and true to the Scriptures and at the same time contend that Christianity can be mixed, adapted or assimilated into other world religions. This faith confronted head-on all other faiths, superstitions, and religions; those who preached it would compromise with no one, the message itself carried the ring of absoluteness and all-inclusiveness. The preaching of *Acts* makes this clear.

The Faith We Obey

Paul opened and closed the letter to the *Romans* with the expression: "the obedience of faith." He wrote of

> the gospel concerning his Son, who was descended from David according to the flesh and designated Son of God in power according to the Spirit of holiness by his resurrection from the dead, Jesus Christ our Lord, through whom we

have received grace and apostleship to bring about the obedience of faith for the sake of his name among all the nations ... (Romans 1:3-5)

He closed the book:

Now to him who is able to strengthen you according to my gospel and the preaching of Jesus Christ, according to the revelation of the mystery which was kept secret for long ages but is now disclosed and through the prophetic writings is made known to all nations, according to the command of the eternal God, to bring about the obedience of faith—to the only wise God be glory for evermore through Jesus Christ! Amen. (Romans 16:25-27)

We are able to watch "the obedience to the faith" in the book of Acts. We have seen the irreducible minimum of the message of *Acts;* there is also an *irreducible minimum* to the *response to that message.* That minimum is faith and baptism. In Acts 2 Christ was preached; the people "received his word" and were baptized. In Samaria "when they believed Philip as he preached good news about the kingdom of God and the name of Jesus Christ, they were baptized, both men and women." (Acts 8:12) The Ethiopian nobleman was told he could be baptized if he believed with all his heart. (Acts 8:26-40) And so with Saul, Cornelius, Lydia, the Corinthians and others.

The irreducible message: Jesus is the Christ, the Son of the living God; crucified, buried, raised, crowned; who alone can reconcile us to God.

The irreducible response: Faith that expresses itself in baptism.

Faithfulness to God demands faithfulness to this message and this response.

Here is the faith that is unique.

Here is the faith that has been battled against through centuries and is battled against even still. But here is bedrock truth that time can never wear away. Here is a sure place to stand. Here is the basis for certainty.

The *sure* message will bring the *sure* response.

Celebrate the Acceptance of One

How can we ever reconcile this fundamental approach with all that has taken place through the years in religion? How can we square it with the multitudes of religious people who might not stand here?

I respond by asking, is this our task? Is our ministry one of explaining the situations as they exist today? Or, is our ministry one of proclaiming the core message? Are we trying to fit institutions together, or are we proclaimers of the kingdom of God?

We do not relate to our world in a political way.

What helps me most is sitting down with one humble person and proclaiming to him the Gospel, watching his heart melt before the grace of our God and his arms open obediently to the Father. It is a profound moment; it is a simple moment. In that moment the uniqueness of our faith reigns supreme. All other moments are in subjection to it.

LIFE: FROM "OUT THERE"

> That which was from the beginning, which we have heard, which we have seen with our eyes, which we have looked upon and touched with our hands, concerning the word of life—the life was made manifest, and we saw it, and testify to it, and proclaim to you the eternal life which was with the Father and was made manifest to us—that which we have seen and heard we proclaim also to you, so that you may have fellowship with us; and our fellowship is with the Father and with his Son Jesus Christ. And we are writing this that our joy may be complete. (I John 1:1-4)

The greatest need of the church is for a deeper commitment to the central truths of our faith. One can be expert at dissecting "gnats" and totally miss the grandeur that lies at the heart of our confession. The one is a joyless, laborious task; the other an inexhaustible fount of joy.

John confronted the first full division in the Lord's body with an uncompromising and thrilling statement of the heart of our faith.

Read the first paragraph again. Two central truths: God has appeared on earth; God has created a fellowship. Two foundation stones. Simple, but profound. They take only three seconds to repeat but cannot be fully grasped in a lifetime.

God Has Appeared on Earth

"That which was from the beginning."
John begins by calling us back to beginnings. The beginning of the faith we preach which grew out of the beginning of the heavens and the earth, and which, in turn, anticipates

LIFE: FROM "OUT THERE"   57

the Beginner of beginnings.

John isn't afraid, is he? He speaks with simplicity and profundity about beginnings which have baffled scientists for centuries.

I can imagine John in a classroom. A professor gets up, and says, "Okay, the question for today is, 'What was in the beginning?' " Immediately, John's hand shoots up. He waves it wildly and eagerly. His is the only hand up. The professor glances uncomfortably his way. With a twinge of impatience, he says, "John, what is it?"

John says, "I know what was in the beginning."

"You do?"

"Oh, yes. Life was in the beginning. And love. And light. Spirit." (John 1:1-5; I John 1:1-4; 1:5, 4:16; John 4:24)

What an answer! How much sense it makes! What's in the beginning? Life, of course. It fits best with everything we've learned that is scientifically certain. It removes one of the greatest problems, that of getting from non-living to living.

And it shouldn't come as any great shock. After all, we're spending millions and millions of dollars every year searching beyond planet earth for *life!*

Recently, we put a space vehicle on planet Mars. Why? One reason was to see if life was there. We breathlessly watched as the small mechanical arm reached out to scoop material from the surface of the planet for us to study. Our primary interest? Life.

John's answer rings true to everything we suspect: there is life somewhere other than this planet.

But John puts content in this life that was in the beginning. It was *loving* life. The life that surrounds and infuses the reality we know is loving. It is also *light,* and it brings light to the deepest questions of humanity. It is also *spirit,* which explains why man cannot be defined in pure material terms.

"The life was made manifest."
And, wonder of all wonders, it is life that wanted to come close to man. But more than come close, to enter into *fellowship* with man. Not to come as little green men on flying saucers, but as a person . . . with a name, and who knows our name . . .

You know, it does seem that men and women have always expected life from "out there" . . . It's strange that so many missed it when it came . . .

Was this Life Real?
Could they have missed this life because it was not real? Was it an apparition, an illusion, a dream? This is a crucial question. John knew it was crucial and therefore proceeds to address it in an almost awkward way.

Speaking of that life that appeared from "outside" he says, ". . . which we have heard, which we have seen with our eyes, which we have looked upon and touched with our hands." Here is *Round One.*

Now, *Round Two.* "The life was made manifest, and we saw it, and testify to it, and proclaim to you the eternal life which was with the Father and was made manifest to us." John, are you afraid we don't hear well?

Round Three. "That which we have seen and heard we proclaim also to you."

Apparently, John was afraid we would miss the point. And yet, what a point he is making! He is claiming that Life came from "outside" and made an appearance here. That God has visited our planet. Did He actually touch this reality? John's answer is put within the context of sensory experience. He says over and over, we heard it, we saw it, we touched it, we looked upon it.

His phraseology is interesting: "Which we have seen with our eyes, which we have looked upon . . ." Is this meaningless repetition? Not at all. The first *seeing* John describes is more casual in nature. We saw His body. His appearance. His skin, clothing and actions. The second *seeing* is deeper. It goes beyond the eyes of the face to the eyes of the understanding. To *look upon* Jesus was to study Him, to examine Him, to question, probe, scrutinize.

John knew the magnitude of this event. He knew the skepticism that would surround it, the misinterpretations that might arise. He could not leave his meaning unclear. John and the others were not content with casual appearances or shallow claims. He says they put Him to the test. They *experienced* Him. Yes, of course they were doubtful. If He was who He claimed to be, nothing could ever be the same again.

The verdict: He was real.

I remember visiting the World Fair in Tokyo in 1970. I came with my Japanese friends to the United States Pavilion. The line was enormous, people standing for hours to get in to see the exhibits.

I finally entered. Of greatest interest was one section that featured an object of world-wide curiosity. The crowd around it was huge! I pressed in closer and closer. Flash bulbs were going off. People were shoving and jostling for a closer look. What was the big attraction?

When close enough to see, there it was. Mounted on a pedestal and enclosed in pyramid-like glass was a rock!

People standing in long lines, waiting hours—to see a rock!

But, you see, it was a special rock. It came from "out there." From the moon! We had sent some men on the mission to the moon. They brought back a load of rocks!

And how we gathered round those rocks. Everywhere, the brightest of the world gathered to study those rocks. They were placed in laboratories where tests were made. They were observed and studied every way imaginable. Men had seen many rocks, but these rocks were special. They were "rocks" among rocks.

John says that's what we did with Jesus. He was a man. Like many other men. Yet, He was different. He came from "out there." Was He real? What could be learned from Him? What knowledge did He have? What light could He shed on the mysteries of man and his universe? These were important questions. "We looked upon him." In every way imaginable. And we came away and were convinced: He was God.

Have we "looked upon" Jesus this way? Or have we been content with the casual look? Have we been more preoccupied with our own rocks—ourselves, the things around us? We take Him for granted. He arouses no special interest in our hearts.

I don't want to put down the significance of the moon landing and the moon rock studies. I do want to say that what John points to outshines every other discovery known to humanity. There is nothing that has ever appeared that is this important—if He's who he says He is. Absolutely nothing.

I wish this could bore its way into the inner recesses of our souls. There is no historical fact that is as important as the appearance of God on this planet. Absolutely none.

Reality is Changed
So profound was this fact that the entirety of reality has

been changed forever. Nothing can ever be quite the same again. By coming to this world Jesus has given us an entirely different way of looking at *people,* an entirely new way of looking at *disease,* a new way of looking at alienation and loneliness—a new way to look at death itself. His coming brought new perspective to hope, meaning, values and morals. He has forever changed the whole basic structure of reality.

Those who believe in Him can never be the same. They are changed. They operate from a new beginning point. Old foundations are not important any more. Things that once were considered great are now small. The things in which we once placed our values and worth have long since been overcome by the beauty and power of this Life.

If only the church could perceive the treasure we have. Do we really believe that this Jesus was God?

I believe the strength of our fellowship will depend on how deeply you and I are seized and empowered by this faith—that Jesus has come, that Jesus was God . . .

Do we believe it?

Do you perform your job as one who believes with all his heart that God appeared on earth in Jesus, that He has touched your life with His and that you are forever different?

Does your marriage suggest, absolutely and with no doubt, your constant and overriding faith that Jesus came and filled your life with the life of God?

Do you love your children with this faith and the love it inspires, the hope? Is it the central fact, the fact of greatest value and importance, that you seek to give your children? Is your faith reflected in the time you give your children, the education, the training, the morals, the values—do these suggest beyond doubt your deep and constant faith that

Jesus was God, that He touched your life with His and gave you eternal life?

Do you view yourself with this faith? Is your self-image derived from this? That God loved you and came for you. That He through the blood of His Son has made you forever beautiful? Is this so deep and so compelling that it has overtaken your self-loathing and guilt and insecurity? That He has brought to you the life of His Father and made you His Father's child—the object of His Father's love. Do you believe it?

Jesus is Unique, the One and Only
The point of Jesus' uniqueness is under attack today— perhaps more than any other point. Jesus has been watered down in current thought and theology. He has been reduced to one of several men who have supposedly experienced messianic consciousness. He is Messiah, a Savior, in the sense that Buddha and Confucius and Mohammed were. A Christ-consciousness has filled them all.

This grows out of an attempt to relate, to be charitable, to be free of exclusiveness. But this is a mistake. No, not simply a mistake, but absolute heresy.

Jesus is not like anybody else in the sense of messiahship and sonship. He is unique, exclusive. He and He alone is the Son of God.

But, what about all the world religions? I suppose men and women will always wonder about this question. But that is not the issue now. What we're discerning is the Bible's claim for Jesus. John's presentation of Christ in I John would never allow any sharing of "Christ-consciousness" with anyone else—past, present, future. Not only would it not allow it, but it would brand any attempt to do so as "anti-Christ." (I John 4:2, 3) Man has no choice here. No options are offered. Jesus is the Son of God. Unique. One can hold no lesser view and qualify as a Christian.

Too hard? Never. Buddhist scriptures have every right to define the Buddhist. The Koran can define the Moslem. The Hindu Vedas can define the Hindu. And the Bible tells us who a Christian is. No one has the right to change that definition. The agnostic has no right to define who a Christian is. Nor any leader of any world religion. Nor theologians. Only the Bible.

And the Bible defines the Christian as one who believes, without reservation, unequivocally, uniquely, absolutely, totally and confidently that Jesus—and Jesus alone—is the Christ, the Son of the living God and that salvation is in Him and in no other. That is the faith of a Christian.

Someone says, "That's weak and narrow."

No, it's power. This is the confidence and faith that has already turned the world upside down once. And if you wonder why the world isn't being turned upside down today, perhaps we have found part, if not all, of the answer.

It is the story of this kind of faith that is recorded in Acts. It and it alone accounts for the marvelous dynamism of the early church, how their lives were lifted off the hinges and turned around completely, how their values had been completely changed. Wasn't it their utter confidence that God has touched their lives? That always changes everything.

God Created a Fellowship

This God who appeared entered into fellowship with us. John says we have told you these things so you "may have fellowship with us; and our fellowship is with the Father and with His Son Jesus Christ."

What created this fellowship? The appearance in the world of this life—God's life. God's life creates this fellowship.

What makes the church? What is the glory and power of the church? What accounts for the holiness of the church? Simply this, that God's life has made the church. It is different from every other organism known to human beings.

Fellowship. God's life makes possible real fellowship.

We talk about alienation. And loneliness. And estrangement. Emptiness. Unfulfilled lives. John says the life that fills the heavens, that takes up mountains and hills and weighs them in scales and balances—this life came to where we are to be our Friend. This is incredible! Meditate upon it. These are truths that can be known only through meditation. Be quiet when treading here. Reflect. Let it sink in. Allow it to penetrate to all the implications of your life.

What gives the church its distinction? God's life. What gives character? God's life. What forms our values? God's life. What determines our view of persons? God's life.

That's what we all need—life. We need life. We want to live. We are aware so often that we are not really living. But we don't know how to find the life that is real.

We received a kind of life from our mothers and fathers. But that didn't guarantee quality. It didn't guarantee against greed and selfishness and adultery and murder. We need new life, life that guarantees quality.

Is there such a life? John says there is. There is a life available to persons that is "abundant life." A life that fills our lives full. That overcomes the emptiness within.

Not only is this a fellowship of life, but also a fellowship that spreads this life. John wanted his readers to know this fellowship.

God's life always reaches out to others. That is its nature. Everywhere the Christian goes, the life of God goes. Into

LIFE: FROM "OUT THERE"

offices and factories and grocery stores and schools. All that we touch is touched with God's life. Think of that! We forget who we are and what we do every day. Through us, God's life reaches out to overcome the death that is in the world.

You can never be quite the same toward a boss or a secretary or an employee or the person at the cash register. Christians are different. They have quality. And it is continual and pervasive, steady.

That Our Joy May Be Complete

Where Jesus is, joy is. When He was born, there was rejoicing. Rejoicing over what they could see would be the results of His coming.

"Be not afraid; for behold, I bring you good news of a great joy which will come to all the people; for to you is born this day in the city of David a Savior, who is Christ the Lord." (Luke 2:10, 11)

He would remove barriers to fellowship. He would:

> scatter the proud in the imagination of their hearts, he has put down the mighty from their thrones, and exalted those of low degree; and he has filled the hungry with good things, and the rich he has sent empty away. (Luke 1:51-53)

Ah, yes, He would:

> preach good news to the poor. He has sent me to proclaim release to the captives and recovering of sight to the blind, to set at liberty those who are oppressed, to proclaim the acceptable year of the Lord. (Luke 4:18, 19)

HIS PEOPLE: HIS PRESENCE

HOW THE CHURCH LIVES

The source of renewal is Jesus Christ. He is the Vine who furnishes life to fruit-bearing branches. (John 15:1-11) He is the Head, "from whom the whole body, joined and knit together by every joint with which it is supplied, when each part is working properly, makes bodily growth and upbuilds itself in love." (Ephesians 4:16) When so related to the Head, it "grows with a growth that is from God." (Colossians 2:19b) Renewal is rooted in Jesus Christ.

Human attempts at renewal are inadequate. Better programs, better projects, better advertising, better facilities will not renew the church; human hands cannot renew the church. Mountains of human endeavor can quiver yet yield only a mouse. Human attempts will fail.

Renewal is found in *relationship,* a right and real relationship to Jesus Christ. Short-cuts fail. So do detours. Easy paths lead nowhere. The church must face Jesus. Before Him she must bow in humility and penitence. She must become "poor in spirit" that she might be "filled with all the fulness of God." (Ephesians 3:19)

Only in her poverty can the church know renewed life and strength. Not financial poverty. Not numerical poverty. Not doctrinal poverty. But poverty of spirit. Poverty of self.

The Revolutionary Principle

The church is the body of Christ. "Now you are the body of Christ and individually members of it." (I Corinthians 12:27) Paul further speaks of the "church, which is his body." (Ephesians 1:22, 23)

As Christ's body, the church receives orders from Christ,

the Head. Nourishment is derived from Him. But, the question is—how?

The *how* is not found in rearranging Bible classes, worship periods, group formation. Renewal cannot be mobilized. Nor does the stream of renewal flow from human ingenuity. All such appeals will fail because they do not go deep enough. They at best produce only temporary results while diverting attention from the real issue.

The *how* is found in a revolutionary principle that was announced by Jesus: *We must die to live.*

Jesus accepted this principle for His own life. Of Himself He said: "Truly, truly, I say to you, unless a grain of wheat falls into the earth and dies, it remains alone; but if it dies, it bears much fruit." (John 12:24)

What was true of Jesus is true for His body, the church. In fact, He continued:

> He who loves his life loses it, and he who hates his life in this world will keep it for eternal life. If any one serves me, he must follow me; and where I am, there shall my servant be also; if any one serves me, the Father will honor him. (John 12:25, 26)

Self-denial, cross-bearing and Christ-following are combined.

> Then Jesus told his disciples, "If any man would come after me, let him deny himself and take up his cross and follow me. For whoever would save his life will lose it, and whoever loses his life for my sake will find it. For what will it profit a man, if he gains the whole world and forfeits his life? Or what shall a man give in return for his life?" (Matthew 16:24-26)

Christians are to give themselves as a "living sacrifice."

"I appeal to you therefore, brethren, by the mercies of God, to present your bodies as a living sacrifice, holy and acceptable to God, which is your spiritual worship." (Romans 12:1) The sacrifice is unconscious of itself.

Paul succinctly states it: "For you have died, and your life is hid with Christ in God." (Colossians 3:3)

For the Christian, for the church, the revolutionary principle is the death of self.

Yet, the church seems so alive to itself. So preoccupied. At times neurotic. Attendance. Contribution. Budgets. How desperately she often clings to these. How fearful when down. How joyful when up. Her eyes are so set on herself. Her plans. Programs. Preacher.

Further evidence of the church's preoccupation with itself is fear. Suspicion. We hang on to traditions for fear we will lose our identity. What is the identity of the church? What is tradition? How much of the present church could we do without and still have the church? Renewal must consider the core of the problem. It must reach for the essence. Only then will we recognize tradition.

It is time to move beyond our fear. Time to trust Christ as Lord. It is time to appeal to His word for what is really essential and to cling to that for all we have. But things that are not bound in His word we must not fight for. Cling to the essential but be flexible in other matters.

The church worries about itself. It is fretful. Protective. Fearful for tomorrow. It clings to itself. This betrays the death to self principle taught by Jesus. When the church clings to itself, it will lose itself. Its hope lies in Jesus Christ. The church must cling to Him.

Do we have a selfish church? A church that boasts of her own accomplishments? Her own victories?

And, what about the ego? Whether in an individual or church? Who is at the center? Is a man at the center? To whom do we appeal? Who can be offended? How can there be jealousy? Envy? Pride? Do churches have egos? Is there any rivalry among us?

Oh, how many of our problems can be traced to *live* selves? Men and women who have not died to self. How can Christ rule as Head when men occupy the thrones? How can the church be renewed? Who stands in the way of renewal? When the church is full of itself, it cannot be full of Jesus. Crucify self and Jesus fills full.

Even here there are not easy formulas. No simple solutions. Death is painful. Each man must wrestle with his own soul. He must face himself. He must inquire. At the deep center of his life. Who rules? Self? Or, Christ?

At the heart of renewal is the death of self. It is true of the Christian. It is true of the church. The revolutionary principle of renewal, of life and power, is the death of self. Only Jesus really taught that.

Resources For Renewal

If the death of self is at the heart of renewal, then *Lordship* must be its resurrected life. Paul has a classic discussion of Lordship and its relation to the church in Romans 14.

First, there were problems in the Roman church. Problems over meats and days. Differences of opinion existed. Brethren were divided. The church was threatened.

Brethren were apparently centered on each other. How they scrutinized each other! Examined each other. Criticized each other. Here is a church with its attention centered on itself.

Paul recognized it. Carefully, he lifted their vision. The man who observed the day did so in "honor of the Lord." The one who ate, ate in "honor of the Lord." Those who abstained, abstained in "honor of the Lord." Paul sets the eyes of the church on the Lord. Off of self.

In classic language he continued to give the life-empowering principle:

> If we live, we live to the Lord, and if we die, we die to the Lord; so then, whether we live or whether we die, we are the Lord's. For to this end Christ died and lived again, that he might be Lord both of the dead and of the living. (Romans 14:8, 9)

Christ died and lived to be Lord! To be *Lord*! To *be* Lord!

Does the church have problems? Are there differences? On what basis can they be settled? Only on the acceptance of Christ as Lord. Men who accept that Lordship are drawn closer and closer together. Christ as Lord is the point on which all eyes are set. Christ as Lord is the center. Christ as Lord is all that to which we are all moving. And so we move closer together.

When the church is surrendering to Christ as Lord, she will experience renewal at its deepest level.

Accepting His Lordship means involvement with *His word*. "If you abide in me, and my words abide in you, ask whatever you will, and it shall be done for you." (John 15:7) Our "new nature" is being "renewed in knowledge after the image of its creator." (Colossians 3:10) The "word of Christ" is to "dwell" in us "richly." (Colossians 3:16)

Involvement with the word means strength for the surrendered life. It is health. It is life.

Too often shoddy Bible classes, shallow literature and "unfired-up" teachers are passed off for Bible study. Because a little material that is Bible-flavored has been covered is no assurance of meaningful involvement with the word of God. Something within a person's heart must get involved with something in the word before anything happens. God's word is living, active, sharp, discerning. (Hebrews 4:12) That is what must be experienced.

Overhauling the Bible school department in terms of literature, facilities, aids, methods will not bring renewal. Only teachers who have died to self, who are surrendered to his Lordship and who are themselves deeply involved with God through His word can bring renewal.

The same is true in the pulpit. Is the pulpit selfless? Is Christ ruling—in attitude as well as word? Did selflessness and Christ's rule govern the preparation? Has the life been gripped by God? Have the words been tried in the fires of day by day living? You see, the life is the issue! If the life is dead to self, alive to Christ, then all else flows beautifully. Renewal will be the order of the day.

Uncertainty gives way to certainty when men and women are involved with the word of God. Renewal cannot take place in an atmosphere of uncertainty. For too many years too few lives have declared the knowledge of God. We have been limping. Unsure. Defensive. Protective. But such will not appeal to men. We must speak with authority. With power. Yet always born of an evident relationship with God.

Third, *prayer* is essential to renewal. The selfless, Christ-ruled, word-involved life will utter words to God. Such a life must communicate, beyond the human realm, beyond time.

Christians may need instruction in prayer. If so, why not turn to the great prayer models of the New Testament? For example, the prayer Jesus taught the disciples to pray in Matthew 6. What a prayer! No other single thing has affected my life as deeply as this prayer. The One who knew most about God and most about man put the two together in these brief words. How significant each word! How tragic its history in our lives!

At the heart of the epistles is prayer. Paul prayed. He taught the churches to pray. But, how many churches today are listening? How many churches know the content of Paul's prayers for the church? How many churches are praying them? How many know what they mean when they read them? Are they not at the heart of the needs of the church? Is the stuff of renewal not there? No church can seriously pray these prayers without experiencing renewal and power. These are the models. We are far from them. But we must move closer. And the time is now.

Trite congregational praying must be replaced by prayers born of selfless, Christ-ruled, word-involved lives. Order of service may sometimes be important; but new lives meaningfully involved with God are of greater importance. Renewal of form will not assure renewal of heart.

Worship is also rich in resources for renewal. Worship should pull a man up out of himself. It should lift. It should inspire. It should transform. It should purify.

But worship cannot be programmed. Worship comes from hearts. Hearts who have passed through the fire. Hearts who have wrestled with self. Who have accepted Jesus as Lord. Who study and pray. Worship must be "in spirit and in truth." (John 4:24)

The dying church has dull worship. People are bored. Nothing happens. The Lord's Supper is abused. So is singing. And praying. And preaching. And giving. Worship is not a form to be observed but an interaction of our spirits with God. If nothing happens in our hearts, have we worshipped? Is the point simply to go or is the point to be changed? Is worship a form to be preserved or a deep spiritual action in which we engage?

How can we talk of renewal until we have met these life issues? Will we not continue to bring to worship our pride, prejudices, traditions, indifference, formality until we have died to self? Self is at the root of the problem. Reading a thousand books on church renewal is unlikely to bring about renewal. We must do the hard work necessary at the center of the problem. And it must reach into all these areas.

When worship is rich in the work of renewal, men and women will have assembled to *reach for God*. In that reach things happen. But, do men understand? Do they come to reach? Do they know to reach?

Fifth, *service*. The church that is serving is the church that is healthy. It undergoes regular renewal of heart and power.

Jesus challenges us: "It shall not be so among you; but whoever would be great among you must be your servant, and whoever would be first among you must be your slave; even as the Son of man came not to be served but to serve, and to give his life as a ransom for many." (Matthew 20: 26-28) Is the church full of slaves and servants? Or, is it full of people who want to sit at the right hand and at the left?

Here again we are at the heart of the revolutionary principle with which we began—the death of self. Only those who have died to themselves will serve others genuinely.

In the congregation of which you are a part who is the greatest? Who is the greatest? What person would you name? Applying the words of Jesus would the first be last and the last first? Who is the greatest? Are Christians seeking greatness along the lines of service? Or, brotherhood papers? Or, offices? Or, a place up front?

Has our spirit of service taken us into the "highways and byways"? Are we bidding sinners to come in? Hair and all? Dirt and all? Welfare and all?

HOW THE CHURCH LIVES

Is our service dependent on our seeing revolutionary changes taking place in the lives of everyone we serve? If so, do we not have our reward? Do we serve for the sake of Christ? Or do we serve to satisfy ego?

Do our worship periods indicate the fruits of service? In those who attend? Are those present from backgrounds very different from our own? Would they be welcome? Could the real sinners get in? Would we be embarrassed? Would we wonder what other brethren would think if they knew we were letting such people attend?

Bring the sinners in and we won't be so troubled about answering questions no one is asking. We won't be plagued with boredom. I tell you it will be exciting! New problems. New questions. We will be driven to Christ. To His word. To prayer. The word of reconciliation will be in evidence. We will learn to live together. To give up our prejudices. And fears. Self will die. Christ will reign. God will be glorified. Sinners will be saved. The church will be renewed.

For renewal, let's open our hearts to the world even as Jesus did. Let's be willing to be stoned, beaten, crucified. Christ suffered. Let's be vulnerable to the blows of the world. Let's venture into the depths of life. Let it try our souls. Let it expose our weaknesses. Tremble. But, run to Christ. Run to the fellowship of Christians.

Let's have done with in-grownness. Withdrawal—begone! Isolation—never! Let's run the risk.

Let the church die to itself. Let's give ourselves away. Our fears. Our problems. "Give, and it will be given to you; good measure, pressed down, shaken together, running over, will be put into your lap. For the measure you give will be the measure you get back." (Luke 6:38) What a principle! What hope for renewal! Give your money away—to others. Give your time away. Give your talent. You possess only what you have given away. Let the church give herself away at all levels and watch her grow. See her joy. Know her peace.

The church is still the place that God wants men to "see what is the plan of the mystery hidden for ages in God who created all things." (Ephesians 3:9) Can men see God's plan in the church? Is it exciting? Is it full of hope? Can men see reconciliation taking place? With God and man? Can men see the love Jesus had for sinners? The selflessness? The courage? The joy? Is the church where it is happening?

How we must love the church. As it is. With its faults and failings. But with its hope. The church is God's plan. The plan is good. It will work.

The crucial issue is: Will I give myself up to Christ? Will I repent? Will I deeply turn from self-rule to Christ's rule? When I am dead to self, Lordship, God's word, prayer, worship and service will flow into my life, into the church, and renewal will happen.

Repentance may be the need. It is the need.

> Put off your old nature which belongs to your former manner of life and is corrupt through deceitful lusts, and be renewed in the spirit of your minds, and put on the new nature, created after the likeness of God in true righteousness and holiness. (Ephesians 4:22-24)

WHEN THE CHURCH IS REAL

How do you explain the sinfulness so painfully apparent in the church? Do we deny it's there? Excuse it? Cover it up? John gets to the heart of "what's real" about the church. He gives us a balanced view, warns us of a fatal trap and urges us to focus on what can be found in the church but nowhere else.

> This is the message we have heard from him and proclaim to you, that God is light and in him is no darkness at all. If we say we have fellowship with him while we walk in darkness, we lie and do not live according to the truth; but if we walk in the light, as he is in the light, we have fellowship with one another, and the blood of Jesus his Son cleanses us from all sin. If we say we have no sin, we deceive ourselves, and the truth is not in us. If we confess our sins, he is faithful and just, and will forgive our sins and cleanse us from all unrighteousness. If we say we have not sinned, we make him a liar, and his word is not in us. (I John 1:5-10)

God Is Light

"For this is the message we have heard from him and proclaim to you, that God is light and in him is no darkness at all."

Now, here's a surprising message: God is light. For much of my life I believed He was largely in the dark. That, at best, we could only vaguely know Him. That we could never expect to know anything about Him with certainty.

The God most people envision is one shrouded in mystery (if not myth). He is distant, aloof and inaccessible.

He is obscured by human images we attach to Him—an old man with long white whiskers sitting yonder on a cloud. An angry, raging, sneering creature who finds great sport in dangling human beings over hot flames. A cold, austere Being of whose love one could never be sure.

The God John knows and presents to us is not like that at all. To the contrary, He is light. He is open, knowable, approachable. He is not in hiding. There is no attempt to trick us or deceive us.

In fact, in His presence the darkness vanishes. Mysteries are made clear. Age-old questions are answered. Perplexities are unraveled. John says,

> I write this to you about those who would deceive you; but the anointing which you received from him abides in you, and you have no need that anyone should teach you; as his anointing teaches you about everything, and is true, and is no lie, just as it has taught you, abide in him. (I John 2: 26, 27)

Have we failed to grasp the "light" God has given us? Do we, as Christians, say "God" with our lips while continuing to walk as if our path were dark?

God enables Christians to know. The simplest servant of God confounds the wisest scientist who does not know God. The "least" in the kingdom of God knows more about what's true and real than the most learned professor who is ignorant of God. The Christian leads the learning of the world. He is always on the cutting edge. He knows the truth without which all knowledge loses its meaning. He knows about the things that will outlast all the studies and discoveries of those without knowledge of God.

The church of our generation has been derelict because we have been afraid of the marketplace of ideas. Men and women who scoff at God but are learned in philosophy, science, psychology and anthropology have had the field of human meaning largely to themselves. They have been allowed to roam free with their own godless concepts of human engineering. Too many Christians have been intimidated into silence.

And this silence does not grow out of the information we don't have in these various fields; it grows out of our own uncertainty of the information that has been revealed.

On matters of most profound importance to every human being the Christian has the only solid information that will ever be discovered. This information does not lead him to pride and arrogance but to a splendid boldness rooted in a servant mind.

This leads us to the nature of our fellowship, the church. The Bible makes clear that the church is a special group, formed by God's life, the dwelling place of God. Those who are members of this body enjoy a unique relationship with God based on an eternal covenant.

Yet, the church on its human side is flawed and sinful. How does the church on the one hand provide leadership in matters of greatest importance to humanity while on the other partake so often of the weaknesses and failures of the flesh?

Is this not the reason for many charges of hypocrisy?

Is this not why many reject our message? They feel our mistakes are too many for us to be credible.

Are not Christians themselves unclear about this question too often?

And among themselves, do not Christians deplore the weaknesses and failures of the church, while among others they are defensive and temperamental?

While arguing for the necessity of the church don't many Christians inwardly suffer from an awareness of the shortcomings of the church?

So often the question is raised: "What do we do with people who are converted? The church we attend is so weak."

The Reality of Sin in The Church

Sin is real in the church. Our only option is to admit it. No defensiveness is needed here; only confession.

John makes this clear.

> If we say we have fellowship with him while we walk in darkness, we lie and do not live according to the truth . . . If we say we have no sin we deceive ourselves, and the truth is not in us . . . If we say we have not sinned, we make him a liar, and his word is not in us. (I John 1:6, 8, 10)

The Church Sins

The consequences of denying we sin are fatal. We "walk in darkness," "we lie," we "do not live according to the truth," "we deceive ourselves," "we make him a liar" and "his word is not in us."

Let's face it: we sin. We cannot say otherwise without denying our very nature. Whatever else can be said about the church, it must be said that the church sins.

What happens when we deny it? The church takes on a different nature from the one God intended.

Deception

We "deceive ourselves" if we deny that we sin. (verse 8)

This is precisely where many in the world believe we are:

a state of deception. They think we've fooled ourselves. They think we have lost our ability to see ourselves. We have left them feeling that we do not believe we make mistakes.

I remember delivering a message on the human side of the church. I pulled no punches. I told the truth about the church.

A brother objected. He felt I had hung out our dirty linen. (In fact, I had not really gone that deeply into our family relationship. I had dealt only with what is very visible to those looking on from the outside.)

I asked, "Did I say anything that wasn't true?"

"No, I guess not."

"Did I say anything the world doesn't already know?"

"I guess not."

"You see, all I was doing was letting the world know that *we* know, that we are aware!"

The next morning there was a knock at my door. A person literally stumbled into the room, crying. She had been in the audience the night before. When the subject was announced, she was extremely angry as she had a long-standing anger directed toward the church. She looked for a way to leave, but because of where she was sitting it was nearly impossible without causing a disturbance.

As the message continued, the very objections this person had harbored all through the years were being stated right out loud in the midst of the church. One by one they were stated, admitted and set in perspective.

The person said she had been unable to sleep all night. She had been wrong all those years. She hadn't understood the real nature of the church.

Two things had affected her: 1) she expected human perfection in the church; 2) she felt the church was held up to being something that it wasn't. It seemed arrogant and self-righteous. Boastful.

Perhaps both things were true. The point is, neither had to be that way.

When the church believes, or leaves the impression, that it does not sin, it only deceives itself. Everyone else knows the truth.

It's time to tell the truth about the church.

Un-reality
A failure to admit sin not only creates a condition of deception, but also a state of un-reality. The church is not real which denies it is sinful. John says we do "not live according to the truth." One of the inherent characteristics of truth is *reality*. Truth is real. Not to tell the truth is not to be real. If there's one thing the world has a right to expect in the church, it is reality.

In the world is illusion; in the church is reality. But, that reality will be present only where there is a confession of sin.

Illusion
Illusion finds its way into the church when we fail to admit our sin. John says "his word is not in us."

We say we go by the Bible. We believe we have His word. We want to live by His word.

Yet, John says if we act as if we have not sinned (or say it outright), His word really won't be in us. We may read His word, we may talk about it, we may preach from its pages;

still, if all of this does not occur among people who are confessing that they are sinful, "his word is not in us."

Nothing is uglier than a group of self-righteous people claiming to have special claim on the word of God. That is illusion of the highest order.

A self-righteous church is deceived, is not real and carries on an illusion. Its true nature has been lost.

The Reality of Jesus in the Church

The reality of sin in the church and the reality of Jesus in the church are not irreconcilable opposites. In fact, they combine to form the real identity of God's people.

Jesus, alone, is without sin.

We, alone, are without Jesus and ruled by sin.

Only if Jesus takes the initiative can we hope to be free from the *rule* of sin.

Here, then, is the mystery of grace in the church.

John puts it this way:

> But if we walk in the light, as he is in the light, we have fellowship with one another, and the blood of Jesus his Son cleanses us from all sin . . . If we confess our sins, he is faithful and just, and will forgive our sins and cleanse us from all unrighteousness . . . But if anyone does sin, we have an advocate with the Father, Jesus Christ the righteous. (I John 1:7, 9; 2:1b)

First, what is the difference between being "in the light" —or in the church—and being on the outside? Is the difference that on the outside there is sin and on the inside there is no sin? No, John has made it clear that those "in the light" must confess their sins. Do those on the inside hold themselves up as sinless before those on the outside? What is the difference? In the difference we see the glory and power of the church.

Fellowship
A fellowship is possible on the inside that is not found on the outside. It is more than a fellowship among persons; it is a fellowship of persons with God. God is the center of the fellowship. "Our fellowship is with the Father and with his Son Jesus Christ."

This is a fellowship that is held together by the strength of God's presence. His strength in our midst breaks down the barriers that divide people. His strength is greater than all the differences that separated us in the world. Greater than national differences, social differences, economic differences, sexual differences. His presence makes us all one.

In the church we are surrounded by people who love us with the love Christ had when He laid down His life for us. "By this we know love, that he laid down his life for us; and we ought to lay down our lives for the brethren." (I John 3:16)

To be in a fellowship where we are loved like this is to be secure.

I know a poor man who was a Christian who became very ill. The illness was expensive. He was helpless. He required constant care. The fellowship met every need. All they had was his. Together it was enough and more to provide for the brother's needs—both financial and personal.

I was talking one Sunday morning to Christians on the power of acceptance in the church. I mentioned our love for the retarded. Following the meeting, I saw a retarded woman approaching me. Her head was lowered, her eyes would hardly meet mine. She spoke in a very low voice. She said, "You know, what you said this morning was really true. Because, you see, I'm a little retarded and no one really cared for me during my life . . . until three years ago . . . when I met these people. You know, they really love me . . . they even let me read."

In a world of alienation and estrangement we all need this kind of love and support and acceptance. That's what you can find in the church.

Forgiveness
We can be accepted in the church because we are forgiven. Jesus' blood is working in His body, the church. It is working to cleanse us from all sin.

The church is not sinless; it is forgiven.

Nothing in all the world is as great as forgiveness. It is the greatest thing that can happen to a human being. It is the most healing thing.

As a little boy, I learned the beauty of forgiveness from my parents. I had told my father a lie at the dinner table one evening. I had gotten away with it . . . I thought. Night fell. Sleep scoffed me. Fear filled my heart. Night after night a tender conscience reminded me of my wrong.

I finally decided death was my lot regardless of what I did. If I didn't tell him, I was going to die. If I told him, he would probably kill me! I elected to tell him.

They were asleep. I awakened them, and, much to my chagrin, they wanted to turn on the light. I confessed with head down . . . and waited for the worst. Instead, I felt strong arms of love surround me. I knew I was forgiven . . . and loved . . . and accepted.

Nothing feels as good as forgiveness.

That's what we have in the church. Not sinlessness, but forgiveness. That's why I'm in the church.

Honesty

In the church you can be honest. You don't have to cover up your mistakes any longer. The masks and disguises can be laid aside. We don't have to pretend we're better than we are. No unreal image to keep propped up. No fear that if anyone ever finds out the real truth about us we'll never be liked again.

No, all that can be laid aside. No more role-playing.

Instead, we can tell the truth about ourselves. We confess that we are not good, that we are not righteous, that we have failed. But, we are surrounded by others who confess the same thing. We are in a group among whom sin is common. But we are in a group among whom forgiveness is also common. Because they've sinned, they won't condemn us; because they're forgiven, they know how to love us.

That's why I'm in the church.

Advocate

And, we have an advocate with the Father. Someone to plead our case. To run to our cry.

I have cultivated a good friendship with an attorney. Just in case! But, more than that, Jesus has offered me His friendship. I'm cultivating it. I need Him. He runs to my cries. Pleads my case before the Father. Assures me I am not condemned.

It's almost as if they look one day, and the Father says, "Would you look at Landon? Did you see what he did? How many times do you suppose he's been told not to do that? I've told him and I've told him and I've told him, and look..."

And the Other One says, "Wait a minute. I love him. He's in me. He's covered by my blood. And if you get him, you'll have to get me."

In other words, the very presence of Jesus is our advocacy. He is our righteousness. He is our wisdom. He is our justification. He is our redemption, Paul says, in I Corinthians 1. He is all of it. And we plead not our own righteousness but the righteousness of Jesus.

He is there as the strong swimmer who, when plunged into the chilly, turbulent waters of life swam successfully, overcoming all temptation and surviving death itself. He stands yonder on the other bank calling us to come after Him and assisting and strengthening us so that we get through the same turbulent waters successfully. Jesus is our Advocate.

A New Life in The Church

Here's the heart of the church then. The heart of the church is the same as the good news of our message. What distinguishes the church from the world? What do we have to say?

Not that we have no sin.

Not that there's never hypocrisy.

Not that there's no failure.

All of that is there. And do you know what we do with one another who sin, are hypocritical and who fail? We love and teach them. Do you have any better idea? Is there any greater approach to these problems? (Only if a brother or sister are completely unresponsive, unrepentant, do we carry out God's will regarding the removal of such a person from our midst.)

No, I'm in the church for a different reason. On the inside, there's forgiveness; on the outside, there's none. On the inside, I can be real and honest. No need to cover up and pretend. On the outside, I must be constantly protecting myself, building walls of defenses, rationalizing my behavior. On the inside, I have a Man in Heaven who pleads for me; on the outside, I am alone, cut off from God.

So, we do not hold up ourselves to the world. We do not preach ourselves.

We hold up Jesus. We preach Jesus.

The provisions God has reserved for us in the church cannot be found anywhere else in the world. "To him be glory in the church and in Christ Jesus to all generations, for ever and ever. Amen." (Ephesians 3:21)

THE FOREVER PEOPLE

The threat of aloneness hangs heavy over our lives, the fear that persons we love will leave us, whether through death, or rejection. As one young woman expressed it to me about her own life: "My life has been a tragedy. It has been departure after departure, pain upon pain, and it's eating my guts out. People constantly run in and out, sometimes caring, but most of the time not. Once I wrote a song: 'You're always leaving and I'm always coming and I don't know which way to be running. Where do I go?' "

No doubt we've all experienced at least a little of this in our lives. Broken relationships. And the loneliness that follows.

This tragedy finds its way into our religious experience. So much pain or disillusionment or broken promises were encountered that you soon wandered away. You quit worshipping. You feel you can't—that you've lost touch. All of that is quite beyond your reach now.

Still, you're not completely comfortable. But you don't know what to do, don't know how to get from the way you *feel* to the point of *doing* something about it. What you'd really like is to feel *right* about yourself again, to feel *right* about your relationship to God. You sense some vague sort of need in the area; but for you, Jesus is pretty far away and you just haven't been able to figure out how to get from where you are to where He is. And you've nearly given up trying.

What you and I need is someone *to be with us*. Someone who'll never walk away from us, who'll never say goodbye. Someone whose presence with us is not conditional on us. Someone who will stay with us in spite of ourselves.

Wouldn't that be strengthening? Can you imagine what it would be like to know you'd never suffer debilitating loneliness ever again? To know you were *with others* in a solidarity that is unbreakable? Doesn't the very thought envelop you, wrap you round with feelings of warmth, love and trust? Let's not give up too quickly.

His Promise

Just before Jesus ascended He called His disciples to Him and gave them these words:

> All authority in heaven and on earth has been given to me. Go therefore and make disciples of all nations, baptizing them in the name of the Father and of the Son and of the Holy Spirit, teaching them to observe all that I have commanded you; and lo, I am with you always, to the close of the age. (Matthew 28:18-20)

Here's the promise: "I will be with you always." What do these words mean? Haven't you heard them before? Haven't you tried to accept them before? Isn't this part of the problem—you once tried to believe, but it didn't work out? You tried to be a Christian but it was a pretty empty experience. You can't say you ever really knew the presence of the Lord in your life. If you thought you could know that, if it could be real, you'd be interested, wouldn't you? What's the problem?

I guess the question is *how*. How will He be with us? Most of us have tried to know the Lord in *special* moments. The times when we felt the Lord was near were times that were special. Maybe it occurred in an assembly of God's people that reached special heights. Things fell together that day, the singing, the praying, the message, perhaps something happened in the midst of the fellowship that touched everyone's heart and brought everyone close together. You felt so close to God. You left wishing it could be that way all the time.

Or you'd been to some devotional. There was a special intimacy that evening. Everyone seemed to love each other so much. Hearts flowed to each other. It was intimate, personal and warm. You fought back the tears. God seemed so near. And you left wishing it could be that way all the time.

Perhaps you'd been on some campaign, a special mission for God. It was intense and concentrated. You felt a deep sense of need because of what you were doing, where you were. The assemblies seemed special. Everyone was on top of the mountain. When you left, you felt like you'd been with those people forever. There were many tears in parting. And you wished it could be that way all the time.

I believe that people sometimes reach out for a special kind of religious experience in an effort to find some tangible sign that would assure them of the presence of God in their lives. Satan tempted Jesus this way. Satan felt that if Jesus were going to trust God as fully as He claimed, He ought to have some visible sign from God which would assure Him of His presence. Jesus rejected that approach. You do not rest your faith in God's nearness on such matters. Faith is not dependent on special experiences like speaking in tongues or some special miracle of healing. This is not the way your Bible directs you into a close relationship with Jesus.

His Presence

Then how does one know the presence of God? Jesus gives at least part of the plan in the words we've read from Him. In a word Jesus says, "You be with me in my mission and I'll never leave you." He ties His *presence* with His *work*. Where His work is being carried out, you can expect to find Him. That's true of the church; it's true of each Christian's life.

Have we ever thought about it in this way? Have we ever raised the question, "How can I know the nearness of the

Lord?" before the word of the Lord, to let it give us its answer? Haven't we sought it more in our *experience* than in the word? Experiences fluctuate; the word is constant. Get the answer from the word, and the hope for stability is greater.

In the verses before us, haven't we used this passage most of the time to prove we must go everywhere preaching the word? Of course, this passage has that in it. But it contains much more than a statement of Christ's authority, a command to go teach, baptize and teach some more. This commission carries one of the most sweeping promises found anywhere in the Bible. It is a promise that speaks directly to the present-day feeling of loneliness and emptiness. It speaks to the sterility many complain about, the dryness experienced in our daily lives. A reality is promised here that each of us desperately seeks. Jesus gives the promise of His presence.

The promise of His presence. Think about that! He will be with us today. He will never leave us. The presence of the Lord wasn't confined to his people in other ages, people who were specially selected for special works.

I think sometimes we read of the presence of the Lord with His people in the Old Testament and quickly conclude that's not for us. Was God closer to His people in the Old Testament than He is to us? Aren't we the ones who are walking in the greatest light? Aren't we the ones envisioned in all the work they did? Are we poorer than those?

Remember how God was with Abraham? And He said to Jacob,

> Behold, I am with you and will keep you wherever you go, and will bring you back to this land; for I will not leave you until I have done that of which I have spoken to you. (Genesis 28:15)

To Moses He promised,

"My presence will go with you, and I will give you rest." Moses replied, "If thy presence will not go with me, do not carry us up from here. For how shall it be known that I have found favor in thy sight, I and thy people? Is it not in thy going with us, so that we are distinct, I and thy people, from all other people that are upon the face of the earth?" (Exodus 33:14-16)

Moses recognized that the presence of God was the mark of their distinction. They were distinct only if God's presence went with them.

To Joshua God said,

"As I was with Moses, so I will be with you; I will not fail you or forsake you . . . Be strong and of good courage; be not frightened, neither be dismayed; for the Lord your God is with you wherever you go." (Joshua 1:5, 9)

To Jeremiah on the occasion of his call: "Be not afraid of them, for I am with you to deliver you, says the Lord." (Jeremiah 1:8)

And now Jesus says to His disciples, as He commissions them: "And lo, I am with you always, to the close of the age."

And we are still His disciples. And He is still with us.

But we ask again, how do we enjoy His presence? Does Jesus not give us the answer in this very context? Have you thought of this passage as giving us, among other things, the basis upon which Christ is with us? And do you believe that if we will follow His instructions, that He will surely keep His promise? Is there anything more sure than that? Let's turn now and see the basis upon which the promise was given.

His Authority
First, to have a close relationship with Jesus we must accept His total authority over all things. Have you thought of this possibility? Especially in a world where everybody

and his brother is trying to tell you what to do, what to believe, where to go, what to buy, how to live your life. Sometimes you get so confused that you don't know to *whom* you should listen. Here's the answer: Listen to the instruction of Jesus. Let Him have the total rule of your life—your plans, your body, your emotions, your dreams. He's the greatest person who ever lived (even by the testimony of His enemies). *He* offers to direct your life.

Have you caught the vision of this possibility? Instead of looking up and seeing a host of people and hearing a myriad of voices, all telling you what to do, that whole stage suddenly clears and one central figure emerges—Jesus, the Son of God, the Son of Man. He knows what a human life should be. And He loves you. He's shown that in His willingness to put His life down for you. So here's One who wants to help you live your life in joy and love, who wants you to know true freedom, who assures that your life will get better as the years pass, instead of worse. The more you think about this, the more appealing it gets. Bringing all of your life and putting it down before Him who loves you, for instruction. You think about that.

His Dream
Second, to those who accept His authority, He offers the invitation to share His dream for the world. He offers you a place in His special company, a place of work and service. "Go spread the news and disciple the nations. People are wandering about over the earth, burdened, numb and without purpose. Go tell them the good news that they can be forgiven, can start life over again, can share in the meaningful work of lifting up those around them, can learn once again how to give a cup of cold water, feed a hungry person, clothe the naked and visit those who are in prison. You learn to live for people."

You could be involved with Him in this kind of work. You could have part in telling others. You want to be close to Him? Join Him in His work and you'll be close. That's a promise, His promise. He has never deserted anyone who was on the field of battle with Him. He is always there.

Union With Him
Third, to be with Christ we must be baptized "in the name of the Father and of the Son and of the Holy Spirit." Jesus is with us in baptism. The New Testament does not tell us of many specific events in which Jesus is always present, but of those it does give, baptism is among them. Jesus and baptism are so close that all of those who have been "baptized into Christ have put on Christ." (Galatians 3:27)

The presence of Jesus is what makes baptism significant. He is there in death, burial and resurrection, the very heart of the good news of forgiveness. Take Jesus out of baptism and it is a mere external action, a church ordinance. Put Jesus in baptism and the heavens rejoice in that moment.

His Teaching
Fourth, we share in the teaching of those who have been discipled. We all become especially attentive to what Jesus has commanded. The reason for this is that in His commandments we find the *secrets* of our humanity. His commandments are the *seeds* of the kind of human life we ought to live.

Many have tried to become human by depositing the wrong kind of seed in their hearts and minds. There are seeds that could make you richer or more famous but not necessarily more human in the right sense of the term; there are seeds that are designed to build your ego—sometimes so big that its weight destroys you. There are seeds that feed you illusions about yourself and what's important in this world. But so many of these seeds fail to lead us to happiness.

In contrast Jesus offers us the right instruction for life. Plant His seeds in your heart and you will grow to be a healthy, productive, happy and joyous person, no matter what the circumstances of your life may be, no matter what the future holds. This is a kind of life that nothing on the earth can destroy or make unhappy. And that's a promise!

I value the instruction of Jesus so much that I let Him call a little staff meeting each morning! In that quiet time I listen to His words of instruction, my orders for the day. He's sent us twenty-seven memos to read and study! If your boss sends you a memo, you read it carefully—very carefully! That's the way I read the memos we've been sent from Jesus. Read them this way and they're more exciting than ever! I even join Him in a working lunch sometimes. We have these sorts of things in the business world—why not in the business of our lives? What better way to spend a working lunch than with one of the memos God sent that tells you how to live?

I'll tell you, you're not alone in this world, at least you don't have to be. We've just forgotten how close a relationship to God we can really have, and what that would mean in terms of the anxieties we carry, the relationships with people we sustain, the questions about our lives that dog our heels. You can hardly imagine how relaxing it is to be free from the burden of trying to preserve the youth of our life, knowing down deep that there is no way we can win (though we go on trying anyway). That's enough to discourage a person! How different to have found some instruction that lets you live each day and each year relaxed, able to enjoy the special pleasures of that time of your life, never having to attempt recovering past life, past dreams, past hopes, past strength, but able to take each day for what it is and live it to the fullest! You can know this kind of life—all of us can.

Jesus gives us four important insights on developing a close relationship with Him: 1) Accept His authority over all things; 2) Join Him in His work of spreading the good news of forgiveness and life; 3) Be baptized in the name of the Father, Son and Holy Spirit; and 4) Be attentive to the instruction and commandments of Jesus.

Is this the way you've attempted to be close to Jesus?

What one or more of those have you left out? Isn't it time to do something about it now?

The Forever People

But, there's still one other aspect of this promise—an exciting aspect. Because Jesus has promised to be with us forever, we are a "forever people." Think that through for a few moments . . . a forever people. That would certainly cure our fear that we will be left, deserted, abandoned by those we love, wouldn't it? The promise is that Jesus will never leave you; and because He has made that promise good, we can say to you, "We'll never leave you." Have you thought of God's family this way? As a forever people, a people who have no plans for ever going out of business, who'll never sell out, or throw a big sale? Because of that, we can say to people every day, "You come over and be a part of us, and we'll never leave you. We'll never go away."

Here's a young mother who's been left alone—two children. That can be a frightening thing. What does she do? Well, we can say to her, "You come over and be with us. We'll never leave you. We'll help you, love you; all that we have is yours. From now on, we're your people. You can depend on us. You can trust us. We're your 'forever family.' "

Perhaps a young person is out there. He or she has had problems at home; relationships have broken down completely; they feel left out and alone. Just tell them to come over to this family. We'll be with them, never leave them out. We'll be with them forever. Isn't this part of what God's family is all about? Isn't this the kind of place, the kind of assurance that people need?

I saw this work recently in the life of a couple I know as very special friends. I had been in school with them several years ago. They had married, had two children, reared them—one is now in college, the other is finishing high school.

Then last year it happened. The doctor informed Sue she was pregnant. Later, during an examination, the doctor said, "Sue, I hear two heartbeats. I want you to go have an X-ray right now." She went. The technician came out smiling broadly and said, "Sue, triplets!" Here's a couple, almost 40, with triplets! How will they handle that? With the help of the forever family they're a part of. A women's class provided them with a diaper service. You can imagine what a relief that was! Others organized and saw to it that she had fulltime help every single day—at no cost. They gave Sue and Lee encouragement and love. They insist on taking the children and freeing both Lee and Sue to spend weekends alone together. It has been beautiful to watch this.

Forever Promises

That's part of what I'm talking about. Still further, Jesus' promise to be with us forever has not only made us a forever family, it has also enabled us to make "forever promises." In *marriage,* for example, people in whom Jesus lives forever can make forever promises. And that's what marriage is, isn't it? "Till death do us part." But not many can make that promise today. There were over one million divorces in the United States last year. Not many people can promise to be with a person till death. Our marriages suffer as a result.

What marriage really is, is two people looking deep into each other's eyes and saying, "Others may come and go in your life but I never will. If you get sick, I'll care for you, feed you, bathe you; I'll do anything for you except leave you. I will never leave you." Because Jesus has promised to be with us forever, we can make that promise to a mate. Our children need to be taught this very carefully. Too many take promises too lightly. They do not know the seriousness of a person's word and promise. As a result, they carelessly make and break promises to their own harm. You can't build a great human life out of broken promises. Our homes will be better when our lives are better. When men know how to be men and women know how to be women, then they have a better chance of being good husbands and wives, mothers and fathers. It's just hard to know how to be a husband if you never learned to be a man. This promise speaks directly to that. If Jesus is with us we're learning what it means to be a man and woman. He knows the pattern and He knows how to accomplish the pattern in a human life. Our tragedy is to be so close to such a resource and not know it.

Friendship is also affected by this promise. Jesus is teaching us what it means to be with a person forever. He has shown us the way to do it. That is why we can now have friendships that never break up, even if the friends are separated and rarely see each other. Friendships based on this promise endure no matter what. "There is a friend who sticks closer than a brother." (Proverbs 18:24)

We're troubled today by "touch and go" friendships. The moment we meet a person—if things go smoothly—we think we have a friend. But friendship is so much more than this. Friends are people who know how to struggle together, who know how to be together and how to be apart, who know how to talk with each other and how to be silent with each other. Friendship is a special gift.

We need deep friendships. Perhaps not too many. I'm of the feeling that we can't really service too many close friends. Quality friendships are based on the deepest commitment. Friends put their lives down for each other. "Greater love has no man than this, that a man lay down his life for his friends" (John 15:13). Do you have a friend who would die for you?

Our *response to Christ* is also molded by this promise. Christ needs disciples who will never leave Him. Disciples who can be depended on.

Near the end of His life, while instructing His disciples, Jesus wondered aloud, "Nevertheless, when the Son of man comes, will he find faith on earth?" (Luke 18:8) His promise is open-ended and unconditional. He has promised to be with us, and He has told us how to be certain of His presence. His presence can make all the difference in how we feel about ourselves, and how we relate to others.

Now, what about us? We can live confidently in His presence. Nevertheless, when the Son of man comes, will He find faith on earth?

THE FLAME OF FIRE

A strong young man, noting the absence of a blacksmith shop in his village, decided to build one. He worked hard, and soon opening day came. Hundreds of villagers came through to wish him well. But there was one problem: No business.

He called on an old wise man of the village. After the old man heard his problem and looked through his shop, he said, "Son, you are strong and well-built for this task. And you have a fine shop here. A fine forge, bellows, anvil and other tools. But you lack one thing: You lack the spark. Without the spark, you can never do the work of a blacksmith."

The prophet Jeremiah knew the value of the spark. It drove him on. "If I say, 'I will not mention him, or speak any more in his name,' there is in my heart as it were a burning fire shut up in my bones, and I am weary with holding it in, and I cannot." (Jeremiah 20:9)

The early church had the spark. They "did not cease teaching and preaching Jesus as the Christ." (Acts 5:42) *Acts* is a history of the spreading flame that finally engulfed the world of that day. Nothing could contain it. It spread in spite of tremendous efforts to subdue it. Kings and governments, rich and poor, wise and unlearned alike fell before it.

Does today's church have the spark?

Look at our brotherhood. We have the finest facilities we've ever had, but do we have the spark? We have more members than ever, but do we have the spark? We have the most money, the most teachers, the most formally trained preachers, the best equipped and staffed Bible schools, the most programs of activities—we have more of everything than we've ever had—but do we have the *spark?*

Are we merely spreading the forms? Spreading the sounds, the pattern? Repeating the marching orders? Simply manning the barracks and going through the drills? Do we have the spark?

Look at our congregation. Is it alive? Afire? Active and real? Examine the worship: Do we know God is in our midst? The work: Does it unmistakably rely on the power of One far greater than anyone or the total of us? The character: Does it bear the imprint of the divine, clearly distinguishing it from every other human gathering? The destiny: Does it without qualification wait for the return of the Lord Jesus? Does the anticipation of His return govern our relationship to each other, to possessions, to values and priorities? Do we have the spark?

Look within our own hearts. Is the spark there? Is your faith real? Are you real? T. S. Eliot said, "We would be ashamed of our most beautiful actions if the world could see the motives that produced them." Do you have the spark?

What if we don't have the spark? Or, what if it is barely lit and flickering? Should we crank up our efforts? Increase our activity? Attend more workshops? Berate ourselves? Change preachers? Attempt to remove the elders? React? Will any of these produce the flame?

No, we must return to Christ, the source. He said, "I came to cast fire on the earth." (Luke 12:49) That fire indicted some and ignited others.

Once, Jesus joined two men on the road to Emmaus. (Luke 24:13-19) He "interpreted to them in all the scriptures the things concerning himself." Later He sat down to bread with them "and their eyes were opened and they recognized him." After He had gone, they said, "Did not our hearts *burn* within us while he talked to us on the road, while he opened to us the scriptures?"

Jesus first ignited the twelve apostles. On Pentecost, the fire imagery is continued as "there appeared to them tongues as of fire." (Acts 2:3) On that day the twelve ignited three thousand. The 3,000 soon ignited Jerusalem. Then all Judea. And Samaria. And on to the "end of the earth." (Acts 1:8)

Years later the fire had cooled in some of the churches. Ephesus had "abandoned the love you had at first." (Revelation 2:4) Pergamum had been influenced by the "teaching of Balaam" and the "teaching of the Nicolaitans." (Revelation 2:12-17) Thyatira was tolerating evil in her midst. (Revelation 2:18-29) Sardis had a false reputation (the church was dead) (Revelation 3:1-6) and Laodicea was lukewarm and self-righteous. (Revelation 3:14-22)

What did these churches need?

They needed the reality of Christ in their midst.

That is the place Jesus began: He began in chapter one of Revelation with a vision of Himself. "John, I want you to take a message to the churches. You can reassure them, first of all, of my living Presence. I am alive. I am real. I have not abandoned them. I am the 'faithful witness.' I am the 'firstborn from the dead,' the 'ruler of kings on earth.' I still love you, will still forgive you, will still make you a kingdom, priests to God."

John turned to see who was speaking. He saw one "clothed with a long robe and with a golden girdle round his breast; his head and his hair were white as white wool, white as snow; his eyes were like a flame of fire, his feet were like burnished bronze, refined as in a furnace, and his voice was like the sound of many waters; in his right hand he held seven stars, from his mouth issued a sharp two-edged sword, and his face was like the sun shining in full strength." (Revelation 1:13-16)

Nothing so arouses a sick church like the vision of the

risen Christ. He is the great physician, the refining fire. His strength makes us well. His presence gives us identity and life. His summons carries us on.

It is sad that we often turn to Him last. We seek initial remedies in other places. We rearrange the furniture. Straighten the pictures. Get a new vacuum cleaner. Stir up more activity. Deliver more blasts.

But all we really need is the living Christ. We need to see Him again. To know He is alive and real. To see and know Him so vividly and powerfully that we sense the fire in our bones and feel the burning in our hearts.

Our fire has no other source. Anything created any other way has no more spark than a flame painted on a canvas.

Years ago a scrap of papyri was found in the sands of Egypt. It is known to us as the *Gospel According to Thomas*. In it are these words attributed to Jesus: "He who comes close to me comes close to the fire."

Peter and John would have related to that. (Acts 4) After listening to them, the rulers "recognized that they had been with Jesus." Their hearts were aflame, and their lives had the characteristics of fire. What are these characteristics?

What is a life like that has been set on fire by Christ?

In the answer to that question, we find the greatest need and hope for churches today.

Fire *is bold*. Those who have been with Jesus are bold. "Now when they saw the boldness of Peter and John, and perceived that they were uneducated, common men . . . they knew they had been with Jesus." Incredible! Men who were bold only through a relationship to Jesus! They weren't regarded as good managers of an economic system. Sharp manipulators. Men who mastered the successful techniques of the business world and who could use religion for profit. Rather, they were men changed by Jesus.

It is exciting to know that Jesus can take any willing person and make him bold for His name. Education, noble birth, good looks, natural talent—none of these is as important as a close relationship with Jesus. So the question is not *who* you are but *whose* you are.

If you're weak, Jesus can make you bold. If you're hesitant, reluctant or fearful, He can make you bold. He brings the "closet disciples" out into public view and opens their mouths. Because Peter and John had been with Jesus, they knew who they were, what they believed and were afraid of nothing.

Second, where fire is, *something happens.* Fire is always active. It never sleeps. Wherever Jesus was, something was happening. Where Jesus dwells in His people, something is happening. There is action and *awareness.*

The rulers could not deny that something happened around Peter and John. No denial stood. A man had been healed and was standing as proof in their presence.

The crying need heard throughout the church and throughout the world today is to see something happen that is of God. That's what we want in the churches; it's what we want in our our lives. What Peter and John did made a difference. We want a relationship with Christ that *makes a difference.* We want a church that *makes a difference.*

No matter what's wrong in our lives, Jesus can change us. The same is true of the churches. Nothing remains still where Jesus moves. He creates disturbance. Activity. There is no "ho-hum" in the life of Jesus: no drowsiness in the life of the early church. Where Jesus is real, things can't help but happen.

Third, fire cannot be *intimidated.* No palace is too fine,

no forest too vast, no city—with its forbidding atmosphere, concrete sidewalks and steel buildings—too frightening. Fire rages on unintimidated, never losing its identity.

Peter and John cried, "Whether it is right in the sight of God to listen to you rather than to God, you must judge: for we cannot but speak of what we have seen and heard." No intimidation here!

The church aflame will never waver before political power structures, religious corruption, poverty or wealth. It makes no such distinctions; it only knows its identity and its mission and it pushes hungrily forward to do it.

Are we afraid of the cities? Are we afraid of Harlem and Watts? Are we afraid of discrimination in all its forms? Are we intimidated by prisons and nursing homes and different races and different languages? Are we fearful of the masses? Do the large and imposing religious structures of our day frighten us?

Will we be driven inside ourselves? Draw a circle around a fire and it will go out. Insulate God's people and you destroy them.

We must not come to a point where we don't know who we are or what we believe. For it is there that we would tremble and fail. Jesus does not stand there; fire does not burn there; we cannot abide there.

I am ashamed that we stand so hesitantly before the scientific world. That we are so reticent before the academically elite. That we are so withdrawn from the centers of debate. It is as if we do not know what is right in the world, where the world is going, or what is important in the world.

Have we forgotten that God has spoken His truth to us? That this truth will be the final arbiter of meaning in this world? Are we so "hung up" on certain abuses in our generation that we have failed to grasp the breadth of God's revelation to humanity?

Have we stopped believing that the humblest person on earth who knows God is greater than the wisest in worldly wisdom? Will we honor the might of the world and hide the secrets of eternity God has whispered into our ears? Will we praise the conferral of degrees while caring nothing for the sonship God has conferred on those who receive Him? Are we confused? Have we forgotten? Do we believe that no man is so high or knows so much or possesses so much as when he stands as a son of God? Intimidate a son of God? Never!

Let us come close to Jesus. Let Jesus rule His church. Only then will the church be what it should be and grow as it should grow!

Fourth, *fire is non-negotiable.* It never compromises itself. It is fire. Always fire.

The disciples of Jesus have a non-negotiable message. We must be careful today lest we stand with a message so diluted that it loses its power, its identity.

Living and teaching in the marketplace of modern society is dangerous. We are tested. Our message is tested. It is grueling. We are forced to question ourselves and our message. Some find it difficult to stand armed with the clearest teachings of the New Testament. Compromise and accommodation often result from these tremendous pressures.

A body of truth is clearly defined in the New Testament. It can be known and defended. No abuse or scrutiny must blind us to the certitude. To be strong and uncompromising with truth does not mean I must be sectarian, legalistic or unkind. Boldness is not synonymous with negativism.

Staying close to Christ secures the proper balance of the message. It keeps prominent what should be prominent. Its focus is sharp and clear. It insures purity of message.

Those who are most faithful to the message today are those who are pressing closest to Jesus. Separate Jesus and the message and the result is grotesque. He truly is the *living word.*

Fifth, *fire cannot be stopped.* Neither could Jesus, Peter or John or the early church.

> "And now, Lord, look upon their threats, and grant to thy servants to speak thy word with all boldness, while thou stretchest out thy hand to heal, and signs and wonders are performed through the name of thy holy servant Jesus." And when they had prayed, the place in which they were gathered together was shaken; and they were all filled with the Holy Spirit and spoke the word of God with boldness. (Acts 4:29-31)

The rest of Acts tells the story. The greater the resistance, the faster it spread. Just like fire. Fan it and it increases.

What are the reasons we give for not growing more rapidly than we do? Are they really the right reasons? Should the size of our membership rolls be the real cause of concern? Isn't the real problem the *nature* of the body? If we were a passionate fellowship, if God were absolutely real in our midst, if the mind of Christ truly ruled, would not most of the problems we're concerned about go away?

What is our real problem? Isn't our real problem our distance from Christ? From the fire?

And isn't the solution found in a return to Him? A real turning of our lives over to Him? Have we really sold out everything to the Lord? Is He central? Does He command you?

THE DISCIPLE: THE CRUCIAL LINK

THE CROSS: TREE OF LIFE

And he began to teach them that the Son of man must suffer many things, and be rejected by the elders and the chief priests and the scribes, and be killed, and after three days rise again. And he said this plainly. And Peter took him, and began to rebuke him. But turning and seeing his disciples, he rebuked Peter, and said, "Get behind me Satan! For you are not on the side of God, but of men." (Mark 8:31-33)

That must have been hard for Jesus to say. He loved Peter a lot, but love sometimes speaks very plainly in the best interest of the loved one.

And he called to him the multitude with his disciples, and said to them, "If any man would come after me, let him deny himself and take up his cross and follow me. For whoever would save his life will lose it; and whoever loses his life for my sake and the gospel's will find it." (Mark 8:34-35)

Real Life: The Cross

Now, I hope that we can get through the familiarity of that verse, down to its real meaning. "Finding life"—that's what we're trying to do. Here is a great teacher, just confessed to be the Son of the living God. He makes a statement about life's aim and life's purpose.

That line speaks as directly to our search today as any in the Scriptures. We are involved in a wonderful, exciting, adventurous search, looking for some answers—not a simple formula to accept, but a cause to give our lives to, a cause worthy of our death. We're right in that search!

So, Jesus says if you would save your life, if you would find life's deepest and richest meaning, then you must lose it. However mysterious that may sound, it is a profound truth. Then He continues, "For what does it profit a man, to gain the whole world and forfeit his life?" (Mark 8:36) You know, that's just common sense. What can I give in return for my life? Janis Joplin said, "You better take care of yourself, because that's all you've got"—before she took her own life.

What does a person gain if he or she gains the whole world but loses his or her life? Now that's a very definite question, isn't it? Jesus doesn't speak in doubt here. When Jesus talks about finding life, losing life and gaining life, He's talking about the tremendous worth of our lives, the importance of our souls. These are relevant issues. When you search for God, you don't look for the trappings of religion. You don't look for some new and novel approach to life. You go with a real question in your heart. You are searching for life. We're searching for an answer to the dilemma of man in whatever century he may find himself.

As we search, let's try to unwrap ourselves from the "over-communication" of some biblical concepts. I think some terms suffer from over-communication. Many of us have heard the words "cross," "church," "salvation," "justification," "sin," "heaven," "hell," "judgment" and all the rest so many times. Maybe we've heard them so much they no longer mean anything.

Somehow, we have to rise above our cultural familiarity with these exciting terms. Let's penetrate them. The wisest people are not those who discover new things; the wisest people are those who find meaning in the familiar. After all, life isn't a huge 24-hour-a-day ecstatic trip. Life is filled with the familiar, the commonplace. Life is filled with things we can seek out readily. The wise person—young person, middle-aged, or older—has eyes which see beneath the surface. They see a pattern, a unity in life.

People are looking for life today—not a cheap thrill. People are inquiring about a new way to go to work, a new way to love a family, a new way to love self, a new way to live. That's what Christ came to bring. He said, "I came that you might have life and have it more abundantly." (John 10:10) Jesus came to give life to persons. We're the ones who put in stained glass windows and hung chandeliers—not Jesus. We're the ones who built the cathedrals; we're the ones who buried His life in ceremony and formality. The way through it is not to grab fire-brands and burn all the buildings, turning out those who have assembled. The way Jesus would deal with it is to speak the truth, even if He died while He was doing it.

That's what the world cries for today. The church cries for people who will just be there and be faithful. Sometimes we get caught up in all of our grand programs, when the only thing God has ever asked of any man is to be there and be faithful. When God can look upon this world and find a faithful person, He can carry out His will. He can do it with one, two or three. The great question today is whether or not there is a man like this available. Can God find a man He can depend on, a man He can trust? He had a few in the first century. He's had a few in succeeding centuries, but where are His men today? He needs men and women who are not too preoccupied with themselves to think of others. He needs people who have learned that life is found when they give themselves away to causes that are higher and worthier. Jesus is talking about that kind of life in this passage.

Artificial Life: Cultural Religion

There *is* such a thing as cultural religion, you know—*status quo* religion. It's an easy, familiar religion. This is religion that makes one feel comfortable. This "cultural religion" you can take or leave. Cultural religion is compatible with whatever a person wants to do with leisure time or in business. Cultural religion tolerates little under-the-table shenanigans. Cultural religion lets people fill up church buildings and deprive the poor and discriminate because of color or economic status—all at the same time. Cultural religion may not be "pure and undefiled" in the care of widows and orphans. Cultural religion may not even express itself in love that brings glory to God. Cultural religion can contain quite a number of egotistical, selfish people. These people will hurt you, run over you, be unconcerned for the people around them. Cultural religion is like an artificial limb—it has no feelings or life. Though it helps a little bit, it has to be strapped on every morning. To go from being religious by culture to being religious by conviction is a difficult, arduous path.

The Cross: The Only Way

The wayfarer,
Perceiving the pathway to truth,
Was struck with astonishment.
It was thickly grown with weeds.
"Ha," he said,
"I see that none has passed here
"In a long time."
Later he saw that each weed
Was a singular knife.
"Well," he mumbled at last,
"Doubtless there are other roads."
(Stephen Crane)

Jesus knew multitudes like that. They loved the ring of His words, the comfort of His presence, but when it came to the way of the cross, they couldn't endure it. "Doubtless," they mumbled, "there are other paths."

We have to be very careful we don't just take a dose of religion. Jesus says the way to follow Him is to die, and you don't die in doses. There's no easy, comfortable way to die.

If a man dies, he dies, and that's it. That's the way of Christ. You can't spread it over with some pretty icing and pretend that's enough. Jesus didn't deal with things that way. He didn't die for nothing. He died because of a tremendous need that men couldn't handle.

What we need as Christians is a faith that is anchored at a central point. We need an anchoring point that has already been through everything we will face. It is precisely at this point Christ places His cross.

You know, I've found in a lot of my preaching I never moved very far beyond the *description* of Calvary. I described the event—the people, the execution, the groans—but rarely touched the height and depth of its meaning. The meaning isn't found in description; it lies beyond the pain of the event itself.

"God was in Christ." Others had been great teachers; others had performed miracles; others had died for people. But Jesus was different. He was God's Son.

Now if Jesus, God's Son, died on a cross and was raised, you can tie to that. There is no enemy or power that can destroy you. You will have come to life with the certainty of never dying. You will have found the pearl of great price.

The Cross And The Church

In the last few years we have had personal struggles in the church. We have been quite distressed that some people decided the church wasn't important. Some of them aren't going anymore. They may have a little group meeting somewhere, and many of those are even fizzling out. They've just decided it isn't very important anymore. These aren't just young people, but people in their 30's and 40's as well. The problem seems to be that everyone can see the Bible teaches that Christ is the head and foundation of the church, that there is a way into the church, there's organization and the like. But—then someone says, "I know all that; my question is, what's it all for?" Do we have a clear answer for that? If we don't have a clear ringing answer backed by fruits, people will say the church is empty, cold, dead.

All of this is founded on misunderstanding. The point is, if we're having that kind of struggle, it's because our message has not come through in pure form. That kind of question never arises when the life of the church is healthy, when it isn't riddled by disease and famine. These questions are raised when the church suffers from spiritual poverty. The response is not to destroy the people who ask the question, but to answer the question. If that means we have to repent, let's repent! If it means we're off center, let's get on center. Let's not back into the corner and feel threatened and intimidated, then come out fighting, unsure what we're fighting about. He who has denied himself and taken the cross *knows* what he is in the church *for.* The church then becomes a great servant body that follows the example of its leader and Lord in laying down its life for its friends. (John 15:13) The church that has the cross at its center is a church that is laying down its life for the world.

The Cross And Baptism

We struggle about baptism. People say, "Well, I just can't see there is any sense in baptism." We assume they're questioning the act of baptism itself when, more often, they're questioning the effect of baptism in our lives.

You may say, "Now, Landon, wait a minute. They don't know what they're talking about, because I've changed." Then they're not talking about you. At the same time we must ask, is everyone like you? Isn't it true many aren't all that excited about what we're accomplishing? Do our lives reflect a people who believe they died and were raised with the Son of God? This is the real question. If the cross is truly central to baptism, then baptism will not be misunderstood nearly as much.

When I understand the cross of our Lord, baptism will suddenly become the most beautiful and most powerful thing in the whole world. No other time in life is more dramatic than when a person is baptized "in the name of the Father, the Son and the Holy Spirit" for the "forgiveness of sins." Nothing greater can happen to an individual. The real problem is the failure to understand what God has done in Jesus Christ at the cross—and its relationship to baptism. It must be clear.

Bumper Stickers and Bad Fruit

The really critical issue is our life and our fruit. If we examine the fruit and find it faulty or diseased, or if we find the tree barren—well, naturally we question the roots. This is what critics of the church are doing, and it's to be expected.

Many are trying to respond to this criticism with things like "bumper sticker religion." But, it won't work. You can stick Jesus on a million bumpers, but until His cross has been taken seriously, it won't change anything in the world. Until I've died and have been raised to give my life for my enemies as well as my friends, then I really haven't been to the cross.

The challenge is that if what we're saying is important and true, then we have to begin the work of giving ourselves for the life of the world. We have to start talking to someone other than ourselves. Why aren't we speaking in the marketplace? Why aren't a few of us getting stoned? Why aren't we getting criticized by others besides our own brethren? What I'm looking for today is a bunch of marketplace sinners who will get after me. Sinners got after Paul. Brethren got after him, too, but sinners got after him. It's time the church moved out into the marketplace. Let her struggle—let her bleed. Let her be attacked. Let her be criticized and censored. If she is the body of Jesus Christ, she will stand. Let's unmask and pull away the disguises, let's stand up and be counted if we believe that Jesus is Christ, the Son of God. Any other kind of religion won't have any force—maybe a little charm—but no force. It may have some sympathy, but it won't help those who are in rebellion and revolt in our world. It won't have real regeneration. It won't see man as one for whom God was willing to give all He had just to find him.

The Essentiality of the Cross

The question we've been asking is this: can you save yourself? If you can, this is all pointless. But if you can't nothing in the world is as important as the redeeming message of Calvary. You see, if God was in Christ at Calvary, it's incredible. It's as though a servant burns up his master's house and business, then when he is called into account, the master says, "No, I'm going to accept all that responsibility and you're free." We've never seen love like that. Sin was totally on the part of man. But God has done something for those who took a wrong turn and are not able to rescue themselves. God on His own initiative loved us while we were yet His enemies. (Romans 5:8) We were yet in rebellion; we were yet in revolt, yet God loved us and gave His Son to die that we might live.

Pyscho-cybernetics might help a few people, but it's not the answer. The Power of Positive Thinking has got some truth in it, but it's not the answer. Neither is Buddhism, and neither is Hinduism, and neither is Humanism. All of them contain some elements that will make our eyes sparkle. But none of them gets into the dirt and slime and scum of where I have to live, then hounds me until it finds me and comforts me, and gives me forgiveness like the love of Calvary. Nothing is quite like that. If we cannot save ourselves, then right now we're looking at an answer. This is the answer.

THE CROSS: THE TREE OF LIFE

Now, I want us to begin seeing how that answer is obtainable. Jesus said here, "If you will follow me, deny yourself, and take up the cross, and follow me." In other words, you've got a poisoned root in your heart. All the good that you want to do, you've found over and over and over that you just can't bring it off. So you live in wretchedness, in agony—or maybe in emptiness.

He says if you would ever be free, then you must deny yourself. We must die with Him that we, too, might come to life by the same power that raised Him from the grave. We are buried with Him in baptism, raised up to walk in this newness of life so we have freedom, joy, peace. It all happens when a man comes to Him and says, "Lord." Then he becomes servant. If you want to get your life together and you want to know unity and peace in yôur life; if you want to be free from those distractions that have wrecked and ruined your life, then accept the answer Jesus gives. Bring the whole thing—emotions, intellect, will, body, speech, eyes, hands—bring the total man—and give them away.

The Creative Principle of the Cross
Senseless? Of course it isn't senseless. It's reasonable. What happens to a kernel of corn if you put it on a shelf? It stays a kernel of corn. What happens to a kernel of corn if you put it in the ground? Why it dies. But then it bursts forth in life and makes hundreds of grains of corn. It's not senseless. It's sensible. It rings true to the law of life.

Christ says a man can have that same kind of experience. He can come to life and become a fruitful branch.

All you have is what you give away. Isn't that true? What about your *breath*? If you quit giving it away, then you've had it! You'll turn blue fast. The only way to keep it is to give it. And try holding in your *love* and see how long you last. You'll be wrinkled, shriveled up, caved in before you know it. The only way to have it is to give it away. The same way with *fire*—the only way for it to burn is for it to give itself away, you see. All kinds of things illustrate this.

So Christ says of us, bring me your whole life as you are. With all your imperfections and with all your mistakes, I have come to take you just like you are. You don't have to be saintly before I will take you. I'll take you just like you are, if you're willing.

You don't get offers like that every day, but that's God's offer of love. By giving yourself away, then, you really find your true identity. Christ offers you an identity—a new name, a new being. He calls you a "servant"—you will become a servant to serve the world. No matter what circumstances you find yourself in, your life will always have meaning, because there will always be someone to serve. The church is the servant body.

When we're frustrated and stressed, a thousand questions are banging against the sides of our skulls; when we wander aimlessly over the land, grown old before our times, and can't cry anymore; it's good news to know that God summoned His holy love and came a long way to find you. He's put us back together, given us a name, a new life and has taken away the burden of sin. He has done it by the way of the cross. To us He has given the key to life—the same pathway, the same cross. To the world He has given the same message, the same hope, the same way to real life.

> But we preach Christ crucified, a stumbling block to Jews and folly to Gentiles, but to those who are called, both Jews and Greeks, Christ the power of God and the wisdom of God. (I Corinthians 1:23-24)

The way of the Cross is Good News.

A FACT OF "LIFE"

"What Do You Seek?"

A passage in John has for several years held a very special meaning for me. It's in the first chapter of the book of John, and Jesus, of course, has become quite well known by this time. His fame has gone throughout the land and He is recognized as an enviable teacher, a disturbing figure, strange in a lot of ways. A person with a quality of life that demanded that you either love Him intensely or hate Him. His life was that holy and pure, that a person just couldn't be passive. One couldn't be indifferent when he was around Jesus. People were intrigued by Him—and many still are.

Some of you have a real desire to believe in Him; you wish that somehow you could reach the point where you could let all of your weight down and really live with Him and in Him, with Him as the foundation of your life. But you're not quite to the point where you can honestly do that with integrity, though you're raising the right questions.

One day there were a couple of men who were wondering about the things we wonder about concerning Jesus. They were following along behind Jesus and all of a sudden they were caught completely by surprise. This great Teacher turned and asked them the deepest question they had ever faced. The question was, "What do you seek?" Or as it is also translated, "What are you looking for?" Now, you know that's really the right question for us. Because we're searching for something. We know we haven't found all the answers about life yet. And so we're still continuing to look; we're probing more deeply into the mysteries of life, hoping to discover the truth of life.

Christ says, "What do you seek?" "What are you looking for?" He got beneath the shallow questions of life. He got beneath the surface questions. He struck deeply into the core and meaning of their lives. Why are you on this earth? What is your life for? What is your humanity all about? What is the destiny of the human race? It was really a tough question.

And they just stood there, stunned, and finally when they could get something out, they said, "Where do you live?" That's kind of an unusual reply to the question, "What do you seek?" Can you make any sense out of that? I think maybe there's this relationship: that maybe in their silence and in their response, they were saying something like, "Jesus, we don't know; that's why we've been following you around. We don't know what we seek. We don't really have our lives put together. We don't really know what it's all about. But we've been listening to you and we've heard about you and we suspect that maybe you know what we ought to be seeking. Could we come and just stay with you for a while, maybe let you talk to us about it?" As Jesus always does, He said, "Yes, you just come." And they went and stayed with Him. What a conversation they must have had!

Jesus Understands Human Nature

The reason the people had this kind of relationship with Jesus Christ is explained in the second chapter of John, where it says He didn't need anybody to tell Him what was in man, "for he himself knew what was in man." (John 2:25) That is, He understood human nature. He understood the frustrations and the desires and the questions of the human heart. He was a summation of all the wisdom of all the ages. He was everything that man has ever sought; that man has ever tried to discover; that man has ever yearned for. He was all of that in one package. He was the fullness of God and was able to say, "When you have seen me, then you have seen the Father." (John 14:9) He was able to say, "I am the way, the truth and the light." (John 14:6) He was able to say, "I have come that you may have life and have it more abundantly." (John 10:10) He was all of this at once. Because He knew what was in man, He understood human nature. He understood that which we seek: the answer for the meaning of our life; a place to stand, a foundation on which to build;

a rule of our heart which is consistent with our humanity and which would bring us the peace, the joy, the freedom and the excitement for which we really yearn. That is what we seek.

Human Nature Is Diseased
It begins with the realization that life is hard, that there are cruel aspects of life, that we are living in a fallen environment. Any way you look at it, we're going to be defiled, we're going to be stained, our systems are going to be poisoned, we're going to lose our heads.

We face the reality of struggle and suffering every day. You can't get away from hospitals. You can't get away from bleeding. You can't get away from pain. You can't get away from suffering. You can't get away from cemeteries. There's no way to escape all of that.

These are things which cry out for an answer; and until we have that answer, then we don't really have the answer for the question of what we seek and what our life is really all about.

We're really looking for some solid place on which we can stand. We're looking for a base for life, a base of meaning, a foundation for life. We are really looking for Jesus Christ . . .

Facing the Truth About Ourselves
You must deal with the problem of yourself. You must deal with your own head and the waywardness of your own heart. You have to deal with your own guilt. You have to deal with your own lack of control, the passions that war in your members. You can't close your mind to all that. You can't write it all off as illusion—because it is real. You must work out relationships at home, whether your home is the finest or the worst in the land. You must make some sense out of that.

Jesus Seeks Us
Jesus understands us. He is the One who shows us our

emptiness and our loneliness and shows us why. He is the same, yesterday, today and forever and is the only point on which we can base our lives. He, when He comes to us, demands that we deny ourselves and take up His cross and follow Him. He demands that in order for us to live, we must die to ourselves. And then in that self that has been yielded to the rule of God, His kingdom can be realized in our lives.

"How Can A Man Be Born When He Is Old?"

> Now, there was a man of the Pharisees, named Nicodemus, a ruler of the Jews. This man came to Jesus by night and said to him, "Rabbi, we know that you are a teacher come from God; for no one can do these signs that you do, unless God is with him." Jesus answered him, "Truly, truly, I say to you, unless one is born anew, he cannot see the kingdom of God." Nicodemus said to him, "How can a man be born when he is old? Can he enter a second time into his mother's womb and be born?" Jesus answered, "Truly, truly I say to you, unless one is born of water and the Spirit, he cannot enter the kingdom of God. That which is born of the flesh is flesh, and that which is born of the spirit is spirit. Do not marvel that I said to you, 'You must be born anew.' The wind blows where it wills, and you hear the sound of it, but you do not know whence it comes or whither it goes; so it is with every one who is born of the Spirit." Nicodemus said to him, "How can this be?" Jesus answered him, "Are you a teacher of Israel, and yet you do not understand this?" (John 3:1-10)

The new birth is perfectly, totally and completely consistent with all of our life needs and with all biblical truths. Pause and think about this line from Jesus: "You must be born again." Suppose you had never heard about the new birth. Suppose you were someone who never knew about Jesus, and then after you had come to know something about Jesus, you still didn't know anything about this. Suppose you were hearing this for the first time: you must be born again, born of water and the Spirit. I wonder what it would do to your mind? Well, it blew Nicodemus' mind completely. And, though I know what he said, I can't figure out what must have been going through his mind when he asked: "How can a man be born, when he is old?" And, as if that wasn't enough, he continued: "Can he enter the second time into his mother's womb and be born again?" I think he must have been excited!

Yet, there is something profound here. He says, you, with all the problems, with all those deep yearnings, you as you are, "must be born again." In other words, you must start over from the first and you do that through the new birth. Denying self, dying to self, renouncing all and coming to a place where the only word that really describes it is a "birth."

When you're born, you're pretty passive. You're totally at the mercy of another. You're totally under the force of another. You're involved, but in a "yielded" way. But it's perfectly and totally consistent with all that Jesus said about the demands for discipleship. A complete and total yielding.

It's like a friend of mine. A very bright person with an excellent education at one of the finest schools in the world. He was telling me the other day about coming to a time in his life when he thought he was losing his mind. I mean literally. He thought he was going to lose his mind in spite of all he could do. He tightened up and consciously tried to hang on because he thought if he ever let go, that would be it! He said he went around for days and weeks and months like that, hanging on for dear life. It was breaking him down completely. His mind was like a flexed muscle. He was just that tight and he was screaming inside. He had so much tension it was like a tight wire. When a wire gets so tight, it reaches the point that you can merely touch it, and it breaks. That's the way his life was wound up. Finally, one day he had reached the point where he could hold on no longer. He would have to let go. He decided to go out into the field to do it. He went out into the field, took one last look all around and said, "I have held on all I can. I'm going to let go.

I'm just going to go over the hill." He got all ready, relaxed and thought it was going to happen in the next second. He didn't know what was going to happen; he just knew he couldn't hold on any longer. So he stopped and totally relaxed, yielded to the possibility of losing his mind. He said he just stood there a little bit. Nothing happened. He said, "Well, go on, go on, can't hold on any longer." I guess he thought his mind would self-destruct! But then, peace came to him. He didn't go, and he said in that moment he began to affirm a kind of life he hadn't known before.

It's similar when Jesus talks about being born again. Life gets so hard. You can get so high strung and so uptight. Whether it's from home or whether it's from school or whether it's from self or whether it's from your own drives or whatever it is, you still don't know what to do. At that point, He says, you must yield. You must be born again.

But how does one do that? What:s really involved in that? Let's work with the word "birth" for a few moments. Jesus chose the word "birth" for a very significant reason. The word birth carried the connotations that would best describe what Jesus knew needed to happen in a person's life. It would cause people to think in the right channels. Nicodemus was really baffled. He was really bewildered. What is birth?

Begetting
First of all, there is the begetting process. Here we are, dead in sin. And, right now, there are people who are saying "we feel dead." Well, the Bible says that's really what it is. It says in Ephesians 2:1: "And you he made alive, when you were dead through the trespasses and sins." Somehow the inner part of your life has gone bad. We experience the death of our spirit.

Jesus said, "I have come that you may have life." How are you going to get that life? You get life through birth. So Jesus said: "The life of God is available to you through birth,

A FACT OF "LIFE"

and if you believe in me, you can have this eternal life. You can have this new quality of life."

But to have it you must be begotten of the Father. He pointed this out in I John 3—that we are begotten by God; that we are born of God. And in I Corinthians 4:15, He says, "You are begotten by the Gospel." And in Luke 8:11, He says, "The seed is the word of God." "You have been born anew, not of perishable seed but of imperishable, through the living and abiding word of God." (I Peter 1:23)

Again, Jesus says, "The words that I have spoken to you are spirit and life." (John 6:63) "For the word of God is living and active, sharper than any two-edged sword, piercing to the division of soul and spirit, of joints and marrow, and discerning the thoughts and intentions of the heart." (Hebrews 4:12) It will get down to where you really live, to where you really hurt, down to where the real pain lies. It is this seed, it is this begetting power that gets down into that part of your nature. And that, Jesus says, is spirit and is life and is power.

So when we are talking about the new birth, we're talking about seed coming into your heart just as seed was present in your physical birth. That seed is defined as the God-empowered word of the Lord.

Notice that it comes to the *inside*. At physical birth you had an objective nature and a subjective nature. One act, the act of physical birth, gave you an objective reality and also gave you a subjective reality. The physical birth gave you a body and gave you a mind. It gave you flesh and it gave you a spirit.

Under the one apex of birth was born the objective and subjective reality of one's life. Now, Jesus says you must be born again, and this new birth will also serve as that one apex from which your objective life will be able to flow and which also will take care of your subjective life. This seed goes into the heart of man, down into all of those subjective problems, into that subjective reality that is in your head. He says it goes down there as spirit and as life and as begetting power, and it begins to operate down there, if the conditions are right. The new birth offers the one unique and really exciting possibility for a man to get his outer life and his inner life together.

Newness
There is something else in birth. New life is expressed. When one is born, he is new. He's coming into existence for the first time. You don't have anything but a name and whatever goes with that name. You come in and you begin to grind out this business of human life. The good news of the new birth is that no matter what condition your life is now in, you can begin anew. The Bible says, "Behold I make all things new." (Revelation 21:5) In physical birth there is newness of personhood, newness of life, newness of individuality and newness of identity. Likewise, in this new birth, there will be that same newness. You start over clean again.

Heredity
When you talk about birth, you are also talking about the glorious process of heredity. You inherit traits and characteristics when you are born. You inherit hair color, maybe a tendency to baldness. (I'm going to drop that right there!)

When you're born of God, you inherit God's qualities. What are these qualities? You read in I John that God is life. So, when you are born again, the life of God comes to your heart. A life that was dead in sin. A life that hadn't been quickened. A life that somehow hadn't really been put together. That longing, that yearning, that tremendous, desperate desire of your heart is realized when you are born again. And the life, the very essence of life, the very core of life, the very Creator of life, the very Sustainer of life comes into your heart, into that empty spot, into that lonely spot, into that void. That's the possibility that's raised. It's what Jesus called "eternal life."

But further. In I John 1:5 we find another quality of God: "God is light." You inherit this *light* of God that shines in the darkness of your heart, that shines into those deep inner recesses of your life and begins to expose and bring to life, that shows you the way out.

You also yearn for *love*. We're all reaching out for love. We're hoping that love will find us. We read in I John 4 that "God is love." When we're born of God, we begin to inherit this great quality, this great characteristic, this nature of God which is *love*.

So if you need *life* in your life, then be born again and you will be given life. If you want *light* in this world, then be born again, and light will be born in your heart. If you want *love* in the world, then be born again and you will find love.

What Shall We Do?

Having taught the beauty and power of the new birth, he next dispatches the apostles to "go into all the world and preach the Gospel to the whole creation. He who believes and is baptized . . ." Now watch the word "baptism" for a moment. He says in Matthew 28:19, "Go therefore and make disciples of all nations, baptizing them in the name of the Father and of the Son and of the Holy Spirit . . ." Baptism in the name of, born in the name of, you see the harmony there, the consistency that's there. In Acts 2:36-38, after a powerful proclamation of Jesus Christ, he brings it to a grand climax and says:

> Let all the house of Israel therefore know assuredly that God has made him both Lord and Christ, this Jesus whom you crucified.
>
> Now when they heard this they were cut to the heart, and said to Peter and the rest of the apostles, "Brethren, what shall we do?" And Peter said to them, "Repent, and be bap-

tized every one of you in the name of Jesus Christ for the forgiveness of your sins; and you shall receive the gift of the Holy Spirit."

Illustrations in Acts

Now, remember Jesus' model—you must be born of water and spirit in order to have new life. Then He says, "I want you to go, preach the Gospel, and baptize them in the name of the Father, the Son and the Holy Spirit." Here are these people who are convinced that Jesus is the Christ, the Son of the Living God and they cry, "What shall we do?" How can we express our faith in that marvelous truth? The reply is instant. By repentance and baptism one comes to the forgiveness of sin.

When you get to the eighth chapter of Acts, many of the Samaritans have had Jesus Christ preached to them and many were baptized. In the same chapter, Philip preached Jesus to the eunuch; the eunuch said, "Here is water, what is hindering me from being baptized?" The same thing is true in the tenth chapter of Acts. Here is the household of Cornelius. "Can any man forbid water that these should not be baptized, who have received the Holy Spirit, as well as we?"

In the sixteenth chapter, Lydia was baptized. In the same chapter, the jailer was baptized. In the eighteenth chapter, many of the Corinthians "hearing, believed and were baptized." In chapters eighteen and nineteen, a man was preaching Jesus. The Bible says he was persuading many men to follow Jesus. We enter the nineteenth chapter, and the question was raised, "Into what were you baptized?" And they said, "Into John's baptism." He commanded them to be baptized "in the name of the Lord." This suggests another significant thing for every honest seeker of truth: even after one is persuaded that Jesus is the Christ, the Son of the Living God, and even though he may be rejoicing in that fact, yet there is still a valid expression of the acceptance of Jesus. Here was a group who had received a baptism, but a baptism that really wasn't a baptism "in the name of the

Father, the Son and the Holy Spirit." Therefore, they were commanded to be baptized in the name of the Lord.

A Contemporary Example

I saw this happen on the continents of Africa and Asia. Someone was pulled out of the fires of some pagan religion who had been bound in fear and superstition; you bring him out before the villagers; the person says, "I'm going to base my life on Jesus. I believe He is the Christ, the Son of the Living God." Then before those watching eyes, that person is born of water and Spirit! That person is buried with Christ in baptism. (Romans 6:4) He is raised through faith in the operation of God. (Colossians 2:12) That is a powerful proclamation of Jesus' death, burial and resurrection. It is beautiful obedience. It forms a clear, concrete, physical, objective line of demarcation that separates the former life from the new life. It becomes a reference point to which the person can always look back, to the very day, the very hour and the very second that he really took that stand for Jesus Christ.

The Drama Of New Birth

Think further about the relationship between the new birth and the death, burial and resurrection of Jesus. He says, "Do you not know that all of us who have been baptized into Christ Jesus were baptized into his death?" (Romans 6:3) You see it is not some act that's separate and apart, something that we are merely doing for the sake of ritual. As a person expresses his faith in Jesus Christ as God's Son, the Bible says he is baptized into the death of Jesus where the powerful, redemptive, cleansing blood was shed; that he is buried with Christ in that baptism; that he is raised to walk in newness of life from that baptism. Here's the place you really draw that line and draw it deep.

But there's one more beautiful, powerful thought that I

want to leave with you about the new birth. Have you ever thought about the difference between life just before you were born physically and life just after you were born physically? Life begins in the womb. But it's narrow, restricted, dark, limited, and it just seems like it would almost be a smothering kind of life in the womb. And then you are born. That's a struggle. It's a real struggle, and there's some suffering there.

You may be weary with life. There may be struggle. As you're thinking about your relationship to the Lord, there will be struggle. There's no other way to be born. Birth involves struggle. And then when the moment of delivery comes, you don't bring anything with you, do you? Naked, a mess, pretty much a mess. That's just the way it is, it's messy. And the passage is so narrow that it will just admit you. Jesus says, the way to life is narrow. He says, it's a straight gate, a narrow gate—not straight like an arrow, but strait as in exacting. It will only admit the yielded person. But then after birth, you can kick your feet and wave your arms, and you're free to keep on growing until you are six feet tall. And some of the fellows reach six feet six and seven and eight and nine—we are wondering when it's going to stop. You know, that's freedom—wonderful, wonderful freedom.

Christ says, "You shall know the truth and the truth shall make you free." (John 8:32) The whole idea of freedom is beautifully wrapped up in the command of the new birth. You must be born again. Just as life before birth was restricted and dark, soon after you were born you came into that same kind of restriction, into that same kind of limitation. And those clouds became dark, and you began smothering inside. You felt your life being drained away. Jesus said, at that point, "You must be born again." If you can really yield yourself, like a little child; if you're not too proud to say, "I want to come into the fullness of life. I'm going to yield to the Lordship of Jesus Christ,"—then you can be born again and experience freedom.

And the things in you—the things in your past, where all the tangles have been—the past is forgiven. There's a deep line that's marked. On the other side is death; on this side you have received life. And, like a little child when it's first born, you know you have room to make your errors. You have room to fall down. You have room to blunder. You have room to knock over a vase. You have room to knock out the glass in the television set. You have room to smear food all over you. You have room, and you have time, and you have a Parent who will work with you and will love you and will care for you. You'll be in a family that will work with you and will love you and will care for you. There will be new life, freedom, real freedom.

No matter how powerfully Satan has strangled your life, we're offering a Savior who has the power to break it all and to leave you free. He does have the power, and so the question is, will I let Him? And you're the only one who can really answer that question.

FREEDOM: WHERE THE SPIRIT IS

For those who live according to the flesh set their minds on the things of the flesh, but those who live according to the Spirit set their minds on the things of the Spirit. To set the mind on the flesh is death, but to set the mind on the Spirit is life and peace. For the mind that is set on the flesh is hostile to God; it does not submit to God's law, indeed, it cannot; and those who are in the flesh cannot please God.

But you are not in the flesh, you are in the Spirit, if the Spirit of God really dwells in you. Any one who does not have the Spirit of Christ does not belong to him. But if Christ is in you, although your bodies are dead because of sin, your spirits are alive because of righteousness. If the Spirit of him who raised Jesus from the dead dwells in you, he who raised Christ Jesus from the dead will give life to your mortal bodies also through his Spirit which dwells in you.

So then, brethren, we are debtors, not to the flesh, to live according to the flesh—for if you live according to the flesh, you will die, but if by the Spirit you put to death the deeds of the body you will live. For all who are led by the Spirit of God are sons of God. For you did not receive the spirit of slavery to fall back into fear, but you have received the spirit of sonship. When we cry, "Abba! Father!" it is the Spirit himself bearing witness with our spirit that we are children of God, and if children, then heirs, heirs of God and fellow heirs with Christ, provided we suffer with him in order that we may also be glorified with him. (Romans 8:5-17)

In developing the theme of Romans 8, there are some things we are *not* going to do. Let's see what those are, so we can lay them aside and get to our main points.

The first thing we're not going to do is get into a semantic tangle. Sometimes when we talk about the Spirit, immediately the discussion gets into complicated word studies. We're going to deal with a perspective.

A second thing we're not going to do is deal extensively with the question of charismatic influences and spiritual gifts. We will assume we have that issue pretty well defined. I do not believe that the miraculous spiritual gifts are operating today in the body of Jesus Christ. I believe they were part of the scaffolding necessary to the development of the New Creation, but not of the permanent structure. I believe a similar scaffolding can be seen in the development of the "original" creation that did not remain a part of the permanent structure. (Genesis 1, 2)

I believe I Corinthians 12-14 sets forth some things that are permanent, some that are temporary. Some "abide"; some "pass away." Some are "more excellent" than others. A careful reading of this material will indicate these differences. Some fall clearly into a category of things that "abide." Some fall equally as clearly into a category that will "pass away."

Furthermore, a careful comparison of the alleged miraculous gifts that are practiced today with the actual exercise of those gifts in the life of Jesus and in Acts shows a remarkable difference. In the New Testament there is an ease that accompanies the gifts, a spontaneity, a certainty—even of opening the eyes of the blind, the raising of the dead—that is missing today. They often occurred almost incidentally in the street, with or without a crowd. Compare that with the theatrics that surround the reported performances of miracles today. I do not believe the practice today has an authentic ring.

Thirdly, we will not deal at great length with the subjective elements of the Spirit's work in a Christian life. We won't go into the detail of how we decide where God wants us to be; whom He wants us to marry; or any of the other vocational and marital matters that sometimes enter a discussion like this. If God has any special plans for us, don't worry. He will get them to us! We don't have to be concerned about that. It's possible for us to demand too much. Perhaps some of us should turn in our resignation as Boss of the Universe, and let God take care of us! Maybe we're still trying to figure out things that are not ours to run. Let's let God tend to that, and let us be His servants to carry out His purposes. The yielded Christian will receive God's will. There's no question about that.

The Center Is Jesus

Romans chapter 8 begins and ends with Jesus Christ. The first and last words are about Him. To know Jesus Christ is to enjoy the gift of the Spirit. To live in union with Christ is to have received the Spirit. Our objective is to do God's will and follow Jesus Christ, not to worry about the Spirit. The Spirit is a gift. You don't become anxious about a gift! If you're going to receive a gift and you start getting nervous and excited about exactly when it's going to happen, how it's going to happen, and you just worry, worry, worry, you take the joy out of the gift. God will give His gifts to those who are in His Son. You don't need to worry about that.

Now with those things aside, let's explore the marvelous scope that Paul has in Romans. The whole of Scripture really develops it. This scope will be tantamount to the establishment of a world view. We want to know where the world is going, where we're going as people in the world. The Lord is painting in great sweeps and broad strokes upon the world's canvas. If we can see those great strokes, a lot of detail will fall into place.

The Spirit: All Encompassing

First of all, let's look at the scope of the Spirit's work.

The Spirit's work today covers absolutely everything, totally. That's how big it is! It's all-inclusive, all-encompassing. It's as wide and as broad and as deep and as high as God's work in Jesus Christ.

Prior to the special activity of the Spirit in the world that is recorded in Acts, God had done many things. The Creation had been formed; part of the promise to Abraham had been fulfilled; Israel had been established and given the law. God had worked through the prophets. All of these things were moving toward the accomplishment of something greater.

Jesus' Work On Earth

> When the time had fully come, God sent forth his Son, born of woman, born under the law, to redeem those who were under the law, so that we might receive adoption as sons. (Galatians 4:4, 5)

When Jesus came, He did marvelous miracles. He made known His teaching. He revealed the God of Abraham, Isaac and Jacob in a way that people had never seen before. He loved in a way people had never known. He had a quality of life—eternal life—which nobody had ever seen before.

He moved steadily toward His death. He went through His trial; was falsely accused, ridiculed and abused, scorned, scoffed at and spat upon. Finally, He was wounded—first, by a crown of thorns and then by nails in His hands and feet. At last, He cried, "Father, into Thy hands I commend my spirit." His side was opened with a Roman spear, and blood and water poured forth. Next He was taken down from the cross. Then followed the burial and the resurrection.

During these days, people were wondering, trying to figure out all of this. All of these mighty things had been done, but nobody quite knew what they meant. No one knew what to do with it. Yes, Jesus died—was buried, and rose again. But what did it mean? Who could put it in the right perspective? Who could apply it to human life? Peter couldn't do it. James couldn't. Neither could John nor Philip. None of them could do it. They could only gather and wait and pray.

So everything God had planned from the beginning of time, everything Christ had made real on this earth, was in abeyance. It was as if the four winds of the earth had been gathered up, and a mighty hush fell over all the universe. Great things have happened—we know that . . . marvelous things; astonishing things; unmentionable, unspeakable, indescribable things have happened. But now what? No one knew what to do.

Acts Two
Then, on the day of Pentecost, Acts 2: "And suddenly a sound came from heaven like the rush of a mighty wind." The winds were held back no longer. Everything has been turned loose. Things begin to happen. It gets exciting! "Tongues as of fire" appear. A message was given and "each heard them speaking in his own language." The people were amazed, disturbed.

Then God's scheme of redemption came into focus. Peter, with the eleven, began saying, "This is what the events of the last several centuries and more particularly, of the last several months, meant."

"This is what Jesus was saying."

"Here's what the resurrection meant."

They began to put it all in order. When that happened, conviction arose in people's hearts and they cried out for the first time, "Brethren, what shall we do?"

It was then the answer was given:

Repent, and be baptized every one of you in the name of

Jesus Christ for the forgiveness of your sins; and you shall receive the gift of the Holy Spirit. (Acts 2:38)

Who pulled it all together? The answer is found in Acts 2:33. Christ had gone back and had sat down on God's right hand and *"having received from the Father the promise of the Holy Spirit,* he has poured out this which you see and hear."

The Spirit Unlocks Mysteries

Who unlocked all those mysteries? It was the Spirit. Who clarified all that God had done? Who defined all God had dreamed? It was the Spirit. Who put all these marvelous things within reach? The Spirit. Who was really doing the teaching? The Spirit. Who was the One who turned loose the power and the life? The Spirit. The Holy Spirit unlocked it all. The Spirit turned loose all of those mysteries, all those plans and dreams.

Everything we enjoy from God as a result of our faith in Christ came through the Holy Spirit. He unleashed it all. It was as if the whole of God's plan suddenly merged to one point, but was contained at that point. None of it could be assimilated. The Spirit then came and unlocked it all. When He did so, it began to spread like a mighty force over the earth.

What would we know today about Jesus Christ, had it not been for what the Spirit had the "holy apostles and prophets" write down about Him? (Ephesians 3:4-6) What would you know about Christ's death and its meaning if the Spirit hadn't explained it? "No man can say, 'Jesus is Lord' but by the Spirit." (I Corinthians 12:4) What would you know about the church? About worship? About forgiveness? We know all of these things as well as the nature of our lives because we're "led by the Spirit."

Those who aren't "led by the Spirit" are floundering— wandering through the streets like the Moon children or the adherents of the Eastern religions. They often reach for God—but without the direction given by the Holy Spirit.

The same is true of people who are trying to repair their lives with "self-help" books, all the "pop-psychology" coming off the press faster than you can keep up with it. But, you see, what few writers know is the real condition of the human race and the real remedy. That's because their minds have not been enlightened by the Spirit. While having some value, these books will never be able to solve the real problem.

The Spirit Brings Life To A Dead World

Let's picture in our minds again, now, the wonderful movement of God's Spirit across the world. At Pentecost, He brings together all of the wonderful things God planned and carried out. Standing there, He looks into the future, where none of those things has yet reached, and He sees hearts that are wide and open and barren. He sees them as they really are. And what He sees is like a great desert. It's sandy, hot, arid. It's parched and cracked, and there is no life. There are no refreshing waters for the human spirit. People's shoulders sag. Their knees are weak. Their eyes are dim. You can look at their faces and tell they're going through the motions of living, but there's no real life there. Then suddenly, the Spirit through the apostles begins churning out this great message—and it washes like a mighty flood out over all that parched, barren land.

Isaiah says:

> The wilderness and the dry land shall be glad, the desert shall rejoice and blossom; like the crocus it shall blossom abundantly, and rejoice with joy and singing. The glory of Lebanon shall see the glory of the Lord, the majesty of our God. (Isaiah 35:1-2)

So here is the marvelous view of God through His Spirit turning loose the Good News as a mighty, refreshing, cool, bubbling stream of water. It begins to flow through the words of His disciples, finding its way into hearts that are empty, lonely, diseased, and torn. Hearts in bondage, enslaved to sin, hopeless. It flows into lives who have lost battle after battle just in the effort to survive. And over that parched and barren land you see a sprig of green here and a pool of water there and a flower blooms yonder. Suddenly some places look like oases. It's life! Where the Spirit flows, there is life. This is where the Spirit fits into all that God and Jesus had done.

The Spirit And The Church

Now secondly, the Spirit starts a flow that is different from what is already operating. Let's think in terms of the flow of the Spirit through the world as opposed to the flow of the flesh through the world. Paul only sees these two possibilities. One is a flow of the Spirit and the other is the flow of the flesh. Now who is in God's flow? I guess that's one of the basic questions we have to answer. Am I part of this thing the Holy Spirit has turned loose? Have I tapped into that? Are its resources my resources? Am I alive? Has it blown across my heart? Has my inflamed spirit been cooled by God's refreshing message of life?

The Spirit and the New Birth
God did not turn the Holy Spirit loose in the world to confuse people, or to divide them. He makes it clear that the message of the Christ must be preached; that upon hearing that message, men and women repent and are baptized "in the name of the Father and of the Son and of the Holy Spirit" for the "forgiveness of sin." Baptism is a birth "of water and the Spirit." It is the beginning of our walk "by the Spirit."

This is a point of some confusion. Some who speak often

about the Spirit speak with confusion about the new birth. How can we ever untangle our views of the Spirit if we are not clear about how one gets into Christ? Few things are taught with greater clarity in the New Testament. We must not be intimidated at this point.

The Church: Dwelling of the Spirit
Furthermore, those who are in the Kingdom of God are in His body, the church. According to Ephesians 2:22, "you also are built into it for a dwelling place of God in the Spirit." The place where a person can enjoy the fruits, the benefits and blessings of the Spirit are in His body, the church. We must not allow the failures of the church at any given moment to blind and confuse us and garble our message. The value and absolute essentiality of the body of Jesus Christ is that God has promised to meet His people there.

Those outside the church are moving in the flow of the flesh. The ones who are in the flow of the Spirit are those who are in the church, the body of Jesus Christ. There is a distinct difference, and there is no way to be out of the church and in the Spirit. There is no way to be out of the church and in the love of God. There is no way to be out of the church and have hope of eternal life. God is in His people. He said, "I will live in them and move among them, and I will be their God, and they shall be my people." (II Corinthians 6:16) We need to be clear. We cannot have great certainty, boldness, confidence until we take our stand on the clear and winning words of the Scriptures that have been preserved for 2,000 years. Here is where we find life in the Spirit. Here are the ones who are in the flow of the Spirit.

Life In The Spirit

Now what's life "in the Spirit" like? What awaits those who are baptized into Jesus Christ and who receive the gift of the Holy Spirit? What awaits those who are in this Kingdom?

FREEDOM: WHERE THE SPIRIT IS

The Spirit is the Answer

We are living in a world where everybody is confused. Conspiracy, something diabolical, is at work. Human life has become the dwelling place of misery, guilt and fear. The human spirit is dead. What's the answer?

If God is not the answer, is there an answer? A man is born into this world, lives in pain and misery and dies without hope. There's no point in saying, "Chin up. It's not all that bad." It *is* bad. It's terrible! Who's going to give him an answer? The people in wheelchairs, those who are retarded—who's going to give them an answer? Who will answer those whose lives are so messed up they hardly know a day with any peace at all? What is the answer for those who are dying in war, or filling up the cancer and heart clinics of the nation? Those who are trying to minister to hungry, bloated children—who will give them an answer? The suicides in the world—who can answer them? When you cry yourself to sleep every night, who's got an answer?

Listen! The flesh has been trying to answer for centuries. It has not produced a state in which people are free from condemnation and guilt.

And all the while, suffering, disease, crime, and war are going on, God's Spirit and the flow generated by Him has been moving silently and quietly over the earth. It picks up the hemophiliac and gives him the $60,000 that he needs because we love him. It provides someone to carry him around if the operation fails, and he is confined to his bed. We'll just stay right with him until he dies. We'll carry him to the bathroom if that is what he needs. We'll put the food in his mouth if that's what he needs. We'll put the clothes on his back, we'll bathe him, we'll make him feel good. We'll stay with him until he dies. And when he dies, the same Spirit that "raised up Jesus Christ from the dead" is going to give him a glorious body. No hemophilia in Heaven! No wheelchairs or blindness in Heaven! No disease in Heaven! No tears, no sorrow, no death is in Heaven!

The Spirit's Word is Final
Whose word is final over this world—that of the flesh or the Spirit? God's people believe that the Spirit's word is final, not that of the flesh. Those who are in that flow are not condemned. Just to be aware of the nature of this world and to know you're not condemned, that's great!

Furthermore, you are free from "the law of sin and death" by itself. We have been trying to halt that law for centuries, but things are only getting worse. We have been trying with all the skill and genius our imaginations can contrive, and things are getting worse.

The flesh can never give you freedom—never. The flesh has never been able to break the power of sin and death, but the power of the Spirit did! It got Jesus up out of that tomb in a hurry. They didn't have to freeze Him for a hundred years until they got some new parts and then try to thaw Him out and put the new parts in, hoping to resuscitate Him. That's the dumbest thing I ever heard for an answer to death!

The best answer for death is resurrection. That's the best cure. Jesus was a specialist, not in funerals, but in resurrections. You have to decide whether death's word is final or life's. The Spirit taught us that life is going to have the final word—not death.

Life and Peace
Where do we find "life and peace"? Paul, in Romans 8, says if the Spirit is in you, then you know life and peace. You're in this other flow. You know how it's all going to come out.

Not only do you have "life and peace" but you can, through the Spirit, "put to death the deeds of the body." The fact of the matter is, he says, that's our obligation. We are debtors. Because of all these things that God is doing in our world, we are debtors. We are not to walk after the flesh, not to let the flesh give us orders. He here begins to challenge the flesh as the boss of our lives. I don't know about you, but most of my problems have come to me through my body. They've come through my ears, my eyes. They've come through my tongue, my hands, my feet. I don't know what to do with my body! Most of our lives have been spent with the body directing the head, instead of the head the body. We haven't known what to do with the body; with lust, with passion, with jealousy, with covetousness. We haven't known what to do with feet that were always swift to run errands of mischief.

But by getting into God's flow of the Spirit, I, by faith in Christ, have seen the flesh killed. Fleshly things do not rule this little 140-pound, bony, skinny outfit. No more! You say, "Well, I wish I was like that." Get with the program! You can be. It's not special, it's for everybody. It's a matter of who is controlling. If the flesh is the ruler, then it's bad news. But if we, by the Spirit of God, put to death the things of the flesh, then it's good news. And you can do it!

We do not have to live lives of adultery and fornication and lying and thieving. We do not have to live lives of jealousy and envy and covetousness. We do not have to live with malice. We do not even have to live with death. We have everything in the Spirit's arsenal at our disposal. Turn grace loose, and see what happens to fornication. Turn the power that raised Christ from the dead loose on your jealousy, and see that your jealousy doesn't have a ghost of a chance. If you are fighting with only the power of the flesh, do you think the flesh is going to vanquish the flesh? Do you think Satan is going to cast out Satan? No.

But if we will live in God's flow, then all the riches, instruments, and weapons of God can be brought to bear on these enemies. We'll win—we'll be victorious. We are obligated to do that. Will we be led by the Spirit or by the flesh? We've been too timid in controlling our flesh. We've been too namby-pamby, too whiney. We've used little rubber hammers on it, when what we need to do is turn loose with the power of the cross of Christ. Crucify it! Get tough with it! Stand up for the rights that God has conferred on you. In His name, challenge the powers of darkness. Let Him command them and drive them out of your life.

Sometimes, we sit around here like we're nothing. We're God's sons! Nothing can get to us. Nobody can condemn us. Nobody can separate us. Say it, brother! Say it, sister! Say it, say it. Say it, over and over until you believe it, until it's real, until there's force and energy and power in your life. Then God is going to have a church to work with. Then with that kind of church and that kind of people He'll smite the darkness of the Northeast. He'll strike down the evil in our metropolitan cities. He will invade every campus across the land. Just give Him the people who know how to say "No" to Satan and "Yes" to the Spirit, and He'll do it.

You're in on God's great scheme. You're in God's great flow—and everything that God has going for Him you have going for you.

The way to really understand this world and its people is to see which ones have opened their lives to what God has done through His Spirit. These are the ones who are governed by the power of hope, not hopelessness. These are the ones who are operating by life, not by death.

In Romans 8, it is as though Paul lets us view the whole universe—the whole creation groaning, suffering, in pain. Lots of discord. Lots of harsh notes. Lots of jarring sounds. Who ultimately directs the course of this present reality? Who is really the Director of this cosmic symphony? We have to decide whether the flesh directs or whether God waves the wand.

What every Christian sees is a world that has a lot of darkness, hot tears, sweat, blood, pain, emptiness, loneliness, failure, defeat, and sleepless nights. But we see a world which, because of what God has done, can look up out of the arena and see Jesus. His cheeks were bathed with tears, as one who has walked where we walk, suffered what we suffer, bled where we bleed. But this One was crowned Lord of Lords and King of Kings, and He keeps calling back in gentle tones, "Be faithful, weary one. Be faithful, little children. Stay with me. Live in the flow of what the Spirit is doing in the world. Don't resist Him. Don't quench Him. Don't grieve Him. But yield your lives to God and let Him make you new, and I give you my word that you'll win. You'll be crowned kings and priests forever."

> O Love that wilt not let me go,
> I rest my weary soul in Thee;
> I give Thee back the life I owe
> That in Thine ocean depths its flow
> May richer, fuller be.

THE POWER OF RECEIVING

THE GIFT OF LONELINESS

Are you one of those whom people just forget about? Well, I know the feeling because I've been there. I think it's one of the deepest feelings of loneliness that one can experience. Why do so many of us suffer from loneliness? And what can be done about it? I want to share some thoughts with you about loneliness. Why we're lonely, and what you can do about it.

Loneliness. Even the word sounds empty. And that's the way it makes you feel—empty. How many people today suffer from emptiness? Adding more people is not the answer. We've never had more people on the earth than we have today, and yet we've never had more loneliness. You can be lonely in a crowd. You can be lonely at a party. Oh, outwardly you're smiling, chatting—but inwardly you're hurting and alone. Such feelings may arise from living with someone who just doesn't understand you. Or may even wait five, ten or fifteen years—children leave home, a marriage has gone sour. No one's waiting for you tonight. The phone sits in silence. No one knocks.

The Burden of Loneliness
Thirteen-year-old Carrie knows the feeling—she stares longingly from a bedroom window at a group of laughing young teenagers down the street. She can't seem to get "in" with them. Tears slowly trickle down her cheeks. She hurts inside.

Then, there is Susan. Thirty. Married four years. One son. She told me how well she remembered her wedding day. Her whole world had taken a promising turn for the better. Marriage was going to rescue her from a horrible loneliness she had felt since she left home and gone on her own. She just knew that in the arms of her husband and children she would never be lonely again. But it didn't work out that way. The painful feeling was back. Her marriage was threatened. Something had gone wrong.

I think Susan approached her problem in much the same way that we do sometimes.

Some Wrong Answers
We're lonely, and so we go in search of friends. And when we find one, we almost try too hard—demand too much—get so close that there is no room for either one of us to breathe, and soon your friend doesn't seem as eager to see you coming. First, you see it in his eyes, and pretty soon he is gone.

Or maybe you've gone the party route. One party after another, an endless round of engagements. But even there, at some point everyone goes home.

Maybe you think sex is the answer. You give everything. Surely such intimacy will relieve your loneliness. And for awhile there was ecstacy. Then your partner walked away. And that compounded your loneliness. Perhaps you should make a commitment—a commitment in marriage. Maybe this will supply what sex alone couldn't. So you try that. At first it seemed to do the trick. But then something happened. Strange tensions. And loneliness.

So you have a baby. Maybe the baby can do what everything else has failed to do. But is he the solution? Isn't it wrong to put that kind of demand on a child? From there you try "human growth" seminars. You "psych" yourself up, telling yourself you're great, that you can stand anything. And let's not forget the weapons of education, work, alcohol, drugs, and a heavy accumulation of things. So many solutions, so many tiny bandages that come loose even before the healing begins. And meanwhile, the warring inside rages on, dragging you down. Isn't there another way to deal with this whole problem?

The Gift of Loneliness

I want you to listen to a special thought. Blot everything else out of your mind, and think about this one thing. Here it is: Loneliness is possibly the greatest, most powerful thing that has ever happened to you. A gift, something to be thankful for. Are you still listening? Have you ever thought of loneliness as a gift? You're probably saying about now, "Now hold on, Landon! That can't be. Landon, it hurts. It's a curse. It's a depression that I'm hardly able to crawl up out of. And worse still, my loneliness leaves me feeling useless, without value. Unneeded. My loneliness is no gift!" To which I would like to reply, "You may be wrong." You may not have looked at it from this standpoint. Let's explore it.

You see, loneliness is not really the result of some void in your surroundings. Or even the absence of people. It's not even simply being alone. There's a gross difference between being alone and being lonely. The difference? Fear. Loneliness is often marked with fear, while aloneness can be warm and beautiful. No, I think the real root of loneliness goes deeper. It reaches to the very bottom of your heart. To your relationship with yourself. To your relationship to what is. To the very basis and meaning of all life. *It really leads us to God.*

Now if that surprises you, hold on. Because remember, everything else you've tried has failed. I'm inviting you to take a deep breath and to think with me clearly and deeply. You want to and you can. The ability to think is part of the glory of being a human being. Now what is the real cause of this loneliness that has so stubbornly fastened itself to us. Well, here's what I believe is the real cause. You have been separated from the very source of your life. That's why you feel empty and alone. There's something missing inside you that's supposed to be there.

Out of Your Element

Let me illustrate what I mean: have you ever watched a bird fly so effortlessly that it almost made you envious? I mean, such freedom . . . such harmony between the bird and its element, the air. Or consider the fish in the water. It swims smoothly, gliding through its natural element of water with no resistance, no problems, no snags. But, let's take that bird and plunge him into the water! Now, how does he do? And take that fish out of the water. How is he going to survive on the bank? Are you any longer envious of him as he flops awkwardly and violently? Soon he weakens, then there is an occasional flop, finally he lies still and dies. What happened? Well, you took the fish out of its natural element. And out of its element, it couldn't function. I suspect it would have suffered severe identity problems. I mean, how could a fish laying on the sandy bank possibly know what it is? Is being apart from other fish the problem? No. You could have surrounded him with ten other flopping fish, and it wouldn't have helped. They couldn't communicate. Nothing can really help a fish on a sandy bank.

We often identify more with a flopping fish on the bank than with one who swims freely in the water. You struggle, you gasp for love and friendship, you yearn desperately to be reunited with something or someone, and sense painfully that you're not where you should be, or even want to be. Stranded. You can't find anyone who's like you, who understands you, who can come close enough to you. You feel so apart. You sense your life slipping away. At first you fought back violently, but then with less energy. And now your life-strength seems about drained away. Just a few more desperate lunges, sapping your last reserve of strength, then you resign yourself to your fate. Waiting for the end. Why? Could it be, just could it be that you're living apart from your natural element? What if there's something in you that corresponds with you, that fits you like air to the bird and water to the fish? Do persons have an element?

I believe persons are made for a special relationship with God. Now, we're born physically, but a natural birth doesn't guarantee that we will know who we are or what we're for. It doesn't really prove that you won't be lonely. The life you received from your parents was fine as far as it went; it just didn't go far enough. No human being is ever complete simply with the life he receives from his parents. You see, you were also made to receive the life of your God. Apart from that life, you're like a fish on a sandy bank. The body is there. The external image is there. But something's missing. Too many things keep you from being happy, from being at peace with yourself and others. Something is missing that leaves you perplexed, wondering who you are, and alone. It's painful. And the worrying. And just as water is the only thing that can cure what's wrong with the fish on the bank, God is the only thing that can free you from your predicament of confusion, that wild thrashing about—struggling, gasping, and finally dying. God is man's element. Only in Him can a person become complete, and find freedom, and joy and purpose.

The Bible's Answer
Do you remember the story of Adam and Eve? Now the woman made by God could be with the man to talk with him, to have fellowship with him. Nothing else was made like that. Only man and woman could communicate with God, receive a word from Him and speak words to Him. And it was all so natural and beautiful. They were totally happy. No sin. No embarrassment. No painful self-consciousness, no wondering what it meant to be a man and a woman. No struggling and gasping and dying.

Yet, later in the account, Adam and Eve suddenly were filled with shame, self-consciousness and embarrassment. They fussed with each other, and still later, one of their sons would kill the other. What happened? What went wrong? Why the sudden struggle and pain and loneliness? *They violated the word of their God.* And by disobeying God they broke away from Him, were thrust apart, separated. Away from God they were out of their element—in the same predicament as a fish on a sandy bank.

All of this makes several passages of scripture come alive.

For example, Jesus said, "Man shall not live by bread alone, but by every word that proceeds from the mouth of God." (Matthew 4:4) Persons can't have full life on bread—even whole wheat bread. Persons are made for the word of God. Again Jesus says, "If you continue in my word, you are truly my disciples, and you will know the truth, and the truth will make you free." (John 8:31-32) The Jerusalem Bible translates, "If you make my word your home . . ." The word of God is the element for persons. And it becomes clear when we remember the way Jesus is spoken of. Listen to this: "In the beginning was the Word, and the Word was with God and the Word was God . . . And the Word became flesh and dwelt among us . . . full of grace and truth." (John 1:1, 14) You see, not only did Jesus bring the word of God—He *was* the Word of God. And the word of God, the Bible tells us, is alive, and in Jesus is life.

To live in Jesus is to live in life. When a fish lives in water, he is complete as a fish. And when a person lives in Christ, he is complete as a person. You see how this relates to the whole problem of loneliness. People are lonely because they're living apart from God. This is the basic cause. This is why they struggle so; why they can't find peace and freedom. It's why friends, sex, marriage, children, work, drugs and alcohol can't cure loneliness. Nothing you could do to a fish on the bank would help it for long. And nothing you can do for a person who is away from God will help him for long. Just as water is the only remedy for the fish, God is the only remedy for men and women.

Are you away from God?

Receiving the Gift of Loneliness
I began by saying that loneliness could be considered a great gift. For me, it was. I remember a period of time in my own life when I struggled terribly. In fact, I know I struggled terribly with loneliness. At one point it nearly crushed me completely. And yet, it was at that very point that I broke through to a fellowship that now nothing can break. Let me explain.

First, my loneliness told me there was something wrong in my life. In other words, it carried its own message. It took me a long time to hear it, but I finally did. And this is the first step in learning to deal with loneliness. You must hear its message that something is wrong in your life.

Second, I came to realize that the thing wrong in my life was tied to my relationship with God. Loneliness led me to God, and that's why I consider it a great gift. What if I had never heard its message? I work with a lot of people who are lonely, and this is what I encourage them to do first: listen, and try to understand why you are lonely. Don't spend quite so much time running, running, running everywhere, desperately trying to find someone or something that can rid you of it. Instead, invest a little time examining your life, trying to figure out why you were made to be happy. If you're not, you need to find out why, and you need to find it out now.

Third, you must realize the seriousness of the problem. Do you know that nothing is more serious in human life than separation from God? The Bible describes this situation in the most extreme terms. For example, Paul says:

> And you he made alive when you were dead through your trespasses and sins in which you once walked, following the course of this world, following the prince of power of the air, the spirit that is now at work in the sons of disobedience. (Ephesians 2:1-2)

Life apart from God is so serious that it's described with the word "death." And you know it's true.

Death, what is it? Well, it's emptiness, it's loneliness, it's destruction, it's separation, it's all the things that happen to human beings away from God. How would you describe a life that is slowly being drained out—that's being broken to pieces? How could you ever describe that as a life that's alive? No, Paul is right. Death is already at work in our lives, and it makes us feel lonely, separated, empty, unable to relate to others. We must recognize how serious it is. When physical death strikes, people gather around. It's strange that people can walk around for years, dead inside, yet no one gathers around.

Fourth, recognizing the seriousness, you must believe that Jesus is your bridge back to God. That's why He came. He came to bring God and me back together again. That's the life He said He was bringing. And no man can come to God except through Him. That's the meaning of the death of Jesus. And the fact that He was willing to die gives you an indication of how serious God felt the problem was. He died for you so you could have the life of God. So you could make friendships.

Do you believe that Jesus is God's Son?

If so, and if you're willing to turn from the lonely life you've lived, with all its mistakes and failures, you can be united with God again. The Bible is clear about how this union takes place. Listen:

> Do you not know that all of us who have been baptized into Christ Jesus were baptized into his death? We were buried therefore with him by baptism into death, so that as Christ was raised from the dead by the glory of the Father, we too, might walk in the newness of life. (Romans 6:3-4)

How are we united with God? Through our faith that leads us to union with Him in baptism. Paul therefore continues, "If we have been united with him in a death like his, we shall certainly be united with him in a resurrection like his." (verse 5) That's the meaning of the beautiful act of becoming a Christian. One comes to see that he's loved by God. He receives that love that expressed itself in the death, burial and resurrection of Jesus. He sees that it was for him. He accepts that, and because of what Jesus has made possible, he dies to his sin and separation from God, and through his faith is buried in baptism with Jesus, is then raised with Jesus, united with Jesus in the true element of human beings—at last.

But, there's even more. Not only are you united with God, but you're also made a part of His family on earth. This means that you'll never be alone again. And if you want to know why this family knows how to stay with you always, it's because Jesus has promised you that "I am with you always, to the close of the age." (Matthew 28:20) Because He is with His family, His family can promise to be with you.

This is one of the greatest promises ever made to a human being. We need people, don't we? People who love us, accept us, forgive us and who will never leave us. And that's the nature of the family I'm talking about now. It's a group of people who've been forgiven so they know how to forgive. A group who were accepted even when they didn't deserve it, so they'll accept you regardless of how much you may have failed. A group whose love is not dependent on what you've done or will do. They will love you simply because you are you. This is important, because if we are loved only when we think we deserve it, then we're in constant jeopardy, fearing we'll do something to cause people to quit loving us. But that's not the case with this family. No matter what you are or what you do, they'll never quit loving you. These people know how to look deep into your eyes and promise you that they'll never leave you, they'll never desert you, never abandon, never go away, you'll never be lonely for want of caring people again.

There it is. In your loneliness, are you able to see the real problem? Your separation from God and from His people.

I met a woman who told me her story. And it was touching. She was in her forties, I suppose. Somewhat shy, had a husband and teenage son. She told me a story of loneliness and fear. She had withdrawn into a house, not even going out for groceries. She sent others. Her fear of people had made her virtually a prisoner in her own home. One day she said the message, part of which I'm sharing now, began coming into her home by means of radio. Each day she listened to a brief radio message that began to reach her. Little by little she began to understand herself and after a year, a friend asked her if she would like to go and hear me speak. Reluctant at first, she finally was persuaded. After a few studies with her, she saw her problem. She really was away from God. Well, she became a disciple of Jesus. Immediately, she began to talk to her husband and son. After several months, her son obeyed the Lord. And about a month later she said with face shining that she had the privilege of watching her son then assist his father in becoming a Christian. Now, she's a part of the family I mentioned earlier—along with her husband and son. Where loneliness and fear once ruled, joy and unity now reign. And, it can happen to you.

For most of us, loneliness is not a choice. It is a reality. But all of us do have a choice—to let loneliness remain a troubling burden, or to find its real value. For those who have chosen the latter, loneliness is a gift.

THE ABC'S OF BEING HUMAN

How can we live truly human lives? What does it mean to be a person? Questions like these elude and frustrate countless thousands today. But answers are available. It is possible to discover the ABC's of being human. I want you to listen to three vital words, because these are the ABC's of being human. They are Awakening, Believing, and Caring: a new beginning, a foundation for your life, and a genuine love that nothing—I do mean nothing—can ever destroy.

I'm wondering whether you've really thought much about your life. Oh, perhaps you reflect on it when someone close to you dies, or during a serious illness; but that's not what I'm talking about. I'm thinking of whether you've really thought through the meaning of your life, whether you've defined your goals clearly, whether you have a plan for your life. Life that aims at nothing usually hits it!

What we need is a map with some directions. Having such a map won't mean you'll never encounter storms or have breakdowns; but it can show you where to find shelter; it can enable you to travel in joy because suddenly your life has a clear direction and destiny.

Most of us map our meaning in words. Beginning with the alphabet you form letters into words, then the words become sentences and the sentences become your life story.

What is your story? Are the sentences coherent? Do you even have the right words? Imagine for a moment that your life is a tray full of letters in a print shop . . . look closely at the letters . . . can you make out the words? Do they say anything about meaning? Purpose? Direction? Destination? Or are they a confused jumble of letters and words that means very little? Will the pressure of living explode your whole print shop, scattering fragments of your life in a thousand directions? Or will the big, black magnet of death one day thrust itself upon you and suck away everything? Is that the way you'll end?

Well, take heart, because it's not too late for the jumble to be transformed into words, *real* words, and meaning. Your life could come together and make sense. But where do you begin? What are the ABC's of being human?

Awakening

The "A" of being human is Awakening. Beginning with your physical birth, you have been traveling from the time when you didn't exist toward a future time when you . . . what? Won't exist again? No, I don't think so.

From *outward appearances* your life is "a spark between one eternal darkness and another." But, our *inward awareness* rejects this. When you die, can you imagine *nothing* taking your place? If being human means ending in pain and nothingness, then what we call life is a rather cruel and purposeless experience for persons who were born to reason and hope and create and love. Don't you think so? If I believed that, I wouldn't be speaking these words, that's for sure. I wouldn't bother speaking any words; words wouldn't make any sense to me.

My life isn't a sick cruelty joke; neither is yours. You're not traveling from nothing to nothing—grinning and dying and crying, sometimes screaming and sometimes silent, and all the time struggling until, finally, you give up the struggle and begin the slow wait until you become nothing again. Life is more than that. God has made it so. A greater possibility awaits you. *It is your mission to find out what that greater possibility is for you.* Let's begin right now.

Awakening: The Discovery of Real Life
Two thousand years ago people were much like we are

now: They didn't understand death; they were afraid it was the final "Z." Then one day, Someone stood up and said, "Don't be afraid, I am the first and the last, and the living one; I died and behold I am alive for evermore, and I have the keys of Death and Hades." (Revelation 1:17, 18)

Could it be? Could this person be the first and last word of your story? "In the beginning was the Word, and the Word was God . . . In him was life, and the life was the light of men. The light shines in the darkness, and the darkness has not overcome it." (John 1:1, 4, 5) Five things are said here: One, Word, or Meaning, was "in the beginning." Second, the Word was God. Third, life was in Him. Fourth, that life was the light of persons who live in the world. Fifth, the darkness in the world could not put this light out!

But what kind of life was this that existed in the beginning? It was *quality life*—that is one of the meanings of the word "eternal." "Eternal life" means quality life. And this quality life came to the earth in the person of Jesus. Jesus brought quality life to human beings.

The claim here is, our world has been touched with a *kind of life* that became the *hope* of all human life. Now let's not miss this. The very question human beings are asking is, "How can we get *quality life?*" We obviously didn't get it from our parents. We received life from our parents, but it carried no guarantee for quality. It did not keep us from stealing, lying, murdering, hating. Parental life was simply not enough. We still grew up confused, empty, lonely in so many instances, living but hardly alive.

How can we get quality life?

We get it from contact with a quality person—Jesus. You say you can't? Of course you can! You've met other people who helped you—gave you a new outlook, a new perspective. I'm talking about the same thing, only on a much deeper level. You meet the person of Jesus. You listen to him. You sense a quality of life in Him you don't have. You come to believe in Him. You accept Him and He gives you new life, a new outlook, a new way of looking at things. Those who have experienced this are called a "new Creation." (Galatians 6:15).

It doesn't occur to most people that the quality life they desperately seek can be found in Jesus. Most people think they would really be living if they just had a million dollars or if they became famous—as if the wealthy and famous of this world are all happy! Most of us pursue the wrong goals. Human beings must awaken to *real* life, life that is stronger than mere physical life, life that can't be "done in" by circumstances around us, but rather triumphs over circumstances. Life that never fades with age but which grows richer by experience; life that doesn't begin in powerlessness and end in fear, but *life* whose deepest characteristics are a sense of righteousness and peace and joy and power (Romans 14:17; I Corinthians 4:20); that is true life, true human life.

Awakening: The Beginning of New Life
This is why enlightened human beings have always insisted that the real hope of a person's life is found in a new beginning, a new birth. We came to life physically because we were touched by the life of human parents; we come alive spiritually when we are touched by the life of Jesus.

A wise scholar once came to Jesus aware that Jesus had unusual perception and insight. Jesus said to him, "You must be born again . . . Unless one is born of water and the Spirit, he cannot enter the kingdom of God." (John 3:5) In other words, a person must awaken to a new kind of life.

I had a friend who had never seen this new birth "of water and Spirit." He couldn't understand at first what it all meant. He wanted to know what the large pool of water was for. He watched in astonishment as a person was taken into the water and lowered gently under and brought up again. What did it mean?

Part of what it means is this: A person—like Nicodemus, one who may even be religious—finds himself imprisoned, unhappy, confused, empty. Then he meets Jesus, that life outside his own. He believes Him, obeys Him. This person goes into the water in faith. And he emerges from the water in freedom, completely unbound from all that meaninglessness and emptiness. He faces the future anew. What is it? It's being born again.

Let's illustrate. A baby is conceived in the mother's womb. For months it lives in darkness, cramped, knotted up —not where one would want to spend his entire life! Then comes the moment of birth. My, the world is big. The cry is heard. The arms and legs thrash. Freedom. But, a few years pass. Again, the darkness surrounds him. Confusion. Life gets cramped. Stifled. Knotted up. Not a way to spend a life! But what can he do?

Is there a *new* birth for you?. Perhaps your life was damaged and scarred in your early years, the years over which you had no control; maybe you made some bad decisions that bogged you down until finally the confusion, the loneliness, the emptiness, the broken relationships were all just too much. Is there no beginning again for you? Jesus says there is. You can—and must—be born again.

A word of caution: I'm not talking about a weak, sentimental, purely emotional formula that says "try Jesus; He's great." Our nation is full of a watered-down, pietistic religious expression that is nauseating. That's not what I'm talking about. This is a tough call to an honest approach to life that doesn't sugarcoat the harsh realities, but instead, enables you to face them head on . . . and win.

So now the question is, can you believe it? Can you believe that you can really begin life again? Is such faith possible? And this brings us to the "B" of becoming human: Believing.

Believing

A popular ad reads: "Something you can believe in." It refers to a car. But you and I know we can't base our lives on a car! We must believe in something more.

What we really need is a reliable foundation for our lives, something significant to believe in. And just as a foundation gives shape to a physical house, what you believe gives shape to your life. Some people build their lives on the thousands of little time-and-possession particles of their everyday existence: What we do. What we have. What we want.

But isn't building on such things like building on the sand? Don't all these little particles have a way of changing rapidly—like the child's castle built in the sand? Jesus said: "A man's life does not consist in the abundance of his possessions." (Luke 12:15)

Others build on whatever their culture hands them: television values; movie morals; pressure ethics. But look at the lives built on these culture values. Are they solid? Do they have quality? Isn't there some other foundation of faith on which we can build?

Listen to what Jesus says: "Everyone who comes to me and hears my words and does them, I will show you what he is like: he is like a man building a house, who dug deep, and laid the foundation upon rock." (Luke 6:47, 48) Jesus says human beings can build their lives on Him and His words. To find this foundation, He says we must dig deep. This makes sense, because how often have we thought we had found meaning and joy only to see it vanish? We hadn't dug deep enough; we laid our foundation on sand.

We dig deep to find a *rock,* a principle or foundation for our lives, a foundation so strong that no storm can destroy us. The catastrophes or daily events, the torrents of our passions—none of these will be able to wreck the life founded on the solid Rock.

Do you believe such a foundation exists? Or are you unable to believe? Do you even know how to believe?

First, never let anyone convince you that believing is abnormal for human beings. On the contrary, without faith we are incomplete as humans. Besides, believing doesn't mean you never have any doubts. True faith doesn't exist on shallow uncertainties or the absence of questions. A man once cried to Jesus: "I believe; help my unbelief." (Mark 9:24)

To believe you must begin where you are. And, you must find the right object for you faith. Jesus is the one you can believe in totally. He has stood the test of centuries. No one has been able to reduce Him. Or eliminate Him. Or even find fault with Him. This is different from believing in religion. Many can't believe today because they don't know what or whom to believe. There are so many religions, so many voices. Listen, you don't have to hear any of them; just listen to Jesus. You can understand what He says. The Bible is *your* book, the handbook for your life. It is your book of instructions on how to be human. You can read it for yourself. It will lead you to real faith in God. "Faith comes by hearing and hearing by the word of God." (Romans 10:17)

I really urge you not to stumble over the perplexities of cultural religion. Just remember that religion and Jesus are not synonymous.

Religion crucified Jesus.

Religion has perpetrated insufferable crimes.

Religion has stifled human freedom.

Religion has practiced the most hideous forms of discrimination.

Religion has defied scientific fact.

To equate Jesus and religion is *fatal*.

For a time I think I made that mistake. I couldn't see Jesus for the religious pollution that enshrouded Him. That was unfair to Him—and fatal to me. With that approach, there was no way I could ever believe.

But, faith in Jesus Christ is different. Faith in Him will give force and energy to your life. It will pull the various elements of your life together and forge them into an incredible unity. It will give you specific goals—right goals, consistent with your nature.

It is this faith that awakens you to the possibility of new birth, of starting over. It is this faith that continues to work in your life, giving shape and power to it everyday, molding you into a beautiful person with a meaningful life who knows why he gets up every morning. It's exciting. And this brings us to the "C" of being human: Caring.

Caring

To be human in the God-defined sense means to be a caring person. All persons were meant to be caring persons. To miss this is to miss our real nature. Jesus was a caring person. Putting your faith in Him will make you a caring person; and you can't imagine how much difference that makes in your life. John puts it this way:

> By this we know love, that he laid down his life for us; and we ought to lay down our lives for the brethren. But if any one has the world's goods and sees his brother in need, yet closes his heart against him, how does God's love abide in him? Little children, let us not love in word or speech but in deed and in truth. (I John 3:16-18)

Are you able to love like that, or have you been hurt so many times that you've erected enough defenses around you that you're protected from feeling? No one can disappoint you because you're going to keep your distance, take care of number one—is that what it means to be alive and human? Can you wall yourself off from people and win as a person? I don't think so.

You must find a way to open yourself to others without leaving yourself vulnerable to destruction. I've found such a way. And I've found it just where you might expect. If the foundation of being human is believing in Jesus, then the place of caring should be with His family, the church. They are gentle to one another, supportive and encouraging. We make mistakes and have problems but we forgive each other. No one holds anything against the others. It's an ideal place to learn to care; and once you've begun learning, you can't imagine how it changes your life. With love and joy and hope—life becomes warm and exciting again. You feel useful and worthwhile. It soon affects everything you do and touch—your home and job and play.

The ABC's of being human. Awakening. Believing. Caring.

Here's how it worked in a woman's life. She was a tragic-looking figure when I first met her—young but tragic. She poured out her heart. Her home was unhappy, husband rarely there, children running loose. Her life had lost meaning. She had tried religion (in an institutional way). She had been a regular church-goer, a spectator on Sunday morning. I began encouraging her to look at *Jesus.* She was introduced to others trying to do the same thing. They encouraged each other. Slowly, she was *awakened* to the possibilities of real change in her life.

Her *beliefs* began to grow. She acted on her faith, was united with Jesus in baptism. She began basing her life on Him.

At the same time she was added to a *caring* fellowship, the church. They nurtured her as she grew, forgiving her mistakes, helping her overcome failures, encouraging her to grow as a person.

Now, three years later, she can hardly believe what has happened. She's a better wife and mother. She's more relaxed and confident. She found a new reason to live. She's a *new human*.

Oh, there have been tears and struggles like before, but now her life had a solid foundation. She knew who she was and where she was going. Therefore, nothing could stop her for long. And some beautiful things have happened to her. Her home has changed. Her relationship with her husband is better; the children are happier. She is still growing.

It can happen to you.

THE POWER OF RECEIVING

"He who receives you receives me, and he who receives me receives him who sent me." (Matthew 10:40)

Have you ever heard a more thrilling statement? So simple, but so profound. It demands that we slow down as we read it. It begs to be sat with, to be reflected upon. Its richness and power come to us most fully in the silence of meditative thought. In that silence our hearts are hushed under its spell. Awe arises. And hopefully, we can never be the same again . . .

A person can receive God. Is this not the greatest statement of human dignity ever conceived? How could the value of a person be stated in more compelling terms?

The presence of God is there when persons meet. Has greater power and worth ever been placed on human relationship?

Jesus says to His disciples, "When a person receives you, that person receives me. I will be there in that relationship. My presence will be there."

Where do you seek God's presence? Do we not seek it in prayer? Do we not seek it in worship? Do we not seek it in special times of devotion? Do we not seek to see His artistry in Nature?

The problem with so many of the ways we seek God is they're often restricted to time and place. One cannot constantly be in an assembly or at a devotional or watching a sunset. We cannot preserve the awe we sometimes feel in these moments—even though we would like to do that.

Jesus suggests another way to experience God's presence—

one that is not restricted to time and place. He suggests a way that can be practiced at work, at school, at home, at the store or wherever we are. There is a way to meet people, Jesus says, that brings God's presence into the moment. I find this potentially revolutionary for the meaning of human relationships.

First, it suggests the enormous value God places on persons. It suggests-the eagerness and the willingness of God to be with persons.

It further heightens the importance of every meeting I have with a person, any person. I can never take the meeting for granted. Familiarity must never obscure the awesomeness of the meeting. Every time I meet a person the possibility of God's presence is there in a unique way. I must not forget that.

Will I Receive Another Person?

Questions are raised at this point: Will I receive other persons? Do I discriminate? Do I prejudge? Do I have several conditions a person must meet before I'll receive him? Do I meet persons with many hidden reservations? Am I condemning of persons?

I feel this is a great problem in the church. Too many people feel scorned by the church. Too many people are being passed over. Too many are prejudged as barren soil.

Without realizing it, many times, we are attracted to people who are very much like us. If they talk like we do, dress like we do, share the same political and economic philosophies that we do, enjoy the same sports, maintain the same basic lifestyle and live with the same values, we are willing to meet them without much hesitation. But, if they're very different . . .

People sense unspoken rejection. They feel it. One doesn't have to tell them they're not wanted; the message will ring loud and clear. The true feelings of the heart cannot be concealed very long.

Persons are not with us in our assemblies and in interpersonal meetings without sensing whether they're wanted or welcome. The casual backslapping, the quick smile, the "we're glad to see you" routine won't convince them. The question is whether we truly want to be with them and whether we truly want them with us. People aren't in search of thirty-second welcomes from others. They can find those nearly everywhere. People are in search of a family. A place to be wanted, loved and accepted. A place where there are people who are genuinely interested in *my story*, who will *listen* to me and *care*.

The receiving of persons is far more significant than we are accustomed to thinking of.

I'm pretty sure it's not our doctrine that people find offensive today. It's not what we teach. *It's us.* It's the people. Doctrine isn't so much in the way (though, of course, it is sometimes the obstacle); *we* are in the way.

In many parts of the country it's not a cappella music, the weekly observance of the Lord's Supper, the practice of baptism for the remission of sins—these aren't really the problem. The problem is our attitude, our shallow judgmentalism.

Do we know how to receive persons? Have we placed the right value on that experience? Do we live in constant consciousness of the importance of receiving people?

What is the basis for our receiving others? Isn't the basis the way God receives us? I should receive another person on the same basis God is willing to receive me.

Does God discriminate? Does the fact that we sin automatically rule us out of God's favor? Must a person be perfect, must he share all the values of God before God is willing to give Himself? If so, would God have ever given Jesus? Would Jesus have ever come to the earth? "But God shows his love for us in that while we were yet sinners Christ died for us." (Romans 5:8) What about the golden text of the Bible?

> For God so loved the world that he gave his only Son, that whoever believes in him should not perish but have eternal life. For God sent the Son into the world, not to condemn the world, but that the world might be saved through him. (John 3:16, 17)

Again, "Those who are well have no need of a physician, but those who are sick; I have not come to call the righteous, but sinners to repentance." (Luke 5:31, 32) "For the Son of man came to seek and to save the lost." (Luke 19:10)

The people could rarely understand Jesus' associations. They asked the disciples, "Why do you eat and drink with tax collectors and sinners?" (Luke 5:30) Jesus Himself answered the objections: "The Son of man has come eating and drinking; and you say, 'Behold, a glutton and a drunkard, a friend of tax collectors and sinners!' Yet wisdom is justified by all her children." (Luke 7:34, 35)

Jesus knew how to receive persons while not condoning the sin a person does. The truth is, there is no other way to receive persons since none come without sin! And, we must receive the person *as a sinner*—not as a person who will soon be rid of all that we object to in his or her life (carrying the unspoken assumption that we'll *really* receive them as soon as they clean up!).

Perhaps the key here is in whether or not we will *give* the person our life. This is the way we know how God relates to sinners: He gave us His life, and He did it *before* we cleaned up.

Will I receive persons today like this?

I remember talking to a mother who had become estranged from her son several years ago. The relationship had deteriorated so that little love could be detected between them. Yet, neither really wanted it that way.

During our conversation, she related the basis on which she was dealing with him. Her rejection had reached the loathing point. She didn't want to see him or his friends. If they came to the house, she made sure they felt unwelcome. The old "cold shoulder" treatment (it is never right for one human being to give another human being the cold shoulder). She wouldn't feed them. Hostility rather than hospitality gripped the home.

She came to see that her approach was not the best one. She was not confronting the sin in her son's life in a human way—much less a God-like way. He was being damaged as a person. She decided to change the basis of the relationship.

The son came home with his friends one evening. They were in the kitchen. She went in and said, "Son, I have a confession to make to you and your friends." They nearly fainted.

She continued, "I haven't been treating you right, and I want to ask you to forgive me. I've been wrong in the way I've rejected you." She went on to discuss this with them. She concluded, "Now this doesn't mean I like or approve some of the things you're doing, but I do love you, and you are welcome here. You're my son."

She left the group of astonished boys and went into another part of the house. They left. She went to bed, but couldn't sleep. Lying there, staring at the darkened ceiling, she wondered if they would interpret her action as approving their ways. Had she given them great license to do wrong?

After midnight, she heard the front door open. The footsteps belonged to her son—no question about it. She had heard them thousands of times.

Then her bedroom door opened and she could see the form of her son silhouetted against the light in the room beyond. He tiptoed across the bedroom, bowed over her and kissed her on the forehead and said, "Mom, I love you so much."

Communication was restored and beautiful things happened in her son's life as well as the lives of his friends. She had begun to receive him as God had received her.

As persons, we need to examine the basis on which we are willing to receive persons. As a church, we need to examine carefully the basis on which we are willing to receive persons. Too much is at stake not to conduct such examination.

Will The Other Person Receive Me?

The next crucial question is whether another person will receive me. "He who receives you receives me." We have dealt with the importance of our attitude toward others, now what about the attitude of others toward us?

I picked up a young hitch-hiker very late one night in a Northeastern city. He was probably 22 years old. He crawled into the back seat and asked me what I did. At 2 a. m. I decided that a very direct approach was in order! "I'm a minister of Jesus Christ."

"Oh, into religion, huh?"

"Absolutely not!"

"Well, you said you were a minister, so that means you're into religion. Right?"

"Wrong!"

I then explained to him the corruption that now characterizes much of religion. I explained how religion played a major role in the execution of Jesus. Only if religion had the same meaning as Jesus could it be said that I was "into religion."

He told me of his sad relationship with religion. How he had "chucked" it all.

After considerable discussion (he had become so involved in the discussion that he missed his exit and we were six miles beyond it! Which only gave us a little more time!), he said, "Tell me how to get into this God."

I said, "I doubt if I could do that. Because you see, I don't even know what you think of me. I don't know if you care about me. I have hurts and fears like you do. Does that matter to you? Also, I'm interested in knowing who you are. What makes you tick. I have an idea you don't have much to go home to at this hour of the morning. Why? I suspect loneliness is a real problem in your life. I'd love to know more about you. Then, if we can relate to each other, I think I can then answer your question more satisfactorily."

He liked this approach.

The point is, how persons relate to and receive one another is so important. God is not divorced from persons. He is not an abstraction that can be known impersonally. God is person. He meets us as person. We meet Him as persons. We meet Him in meeting others. (I John 4:19-21)

Dynamic Relationships

Let's apply these principles to the relationships we have with others.

Marriage
Isn't the problem in many marriages centered in this very principle? Two people start out receiving one another. It is possible that we quit giving and this is perceived as the cause of the breakdown. Perhaps that is true in some instances. But, I suggest that the powerful missing dynamic is an unwillingness on the part of one to receive the other. When I quit receiving, what happens to the presence of God? Is God present when one human being rejects the other? All the religious words and actions in the world cannot preserve the reality of God's presence in the midst of personal rejection. That explains why husbands and wives can keep up a facade of religious words and activities right up to the moment of separation. And we wonder how in the world it could happen. They were so religious. We forget that some of the most religious people in the world are the greatest masters at rejecting persons . . .

Marriages begin to break when one quits receiving the other.

Is an unwillingness to receive ever justified?

Are husbands and wives to receive each other on the same grounds that God receives us? Are irritations grounds for rejection? Apathy? Indifference? Other interests? Does God ever cease wooing us and loving us? Do we not find here the fertile ground of human growth? Do we not become greater as persons when we are faithful to our promises, when we continue to subject to the Lordship of Jesus the feelings that cause us to reject others? In marriage, united in love through a covenant till death, we are provided with the most powerful of all human laboratories for growth. As two people receive each other, they receive the presence of God. His presence is always healing. It binds up wounds, closes gaps and makes us new every day.

Friendship
"Greater love has no man than this, that a man lay down his life for his friends." (John 15:13)

The deepest friendships are the ones ripened over the years by the commitment to receive without limitation.

Friends give and friends receive. "There is a friend who sticks closer than a brother." (Proverbs 18:24)

We often miss the opportunity inherent in true friendship. Friendship offers the opportunity to practice in a unique way the basis of the friendship of God. Friends offer us more latitude in our mistakes before leaving us. We are more secure in friendship. We can be ourselves. We can experience the darker sides of our nature in loving relationship that will not reject us but rather encourage us.

Every person needs friends like this. One must be willing to pay the price of friendship. He must accept responsibility for such a relationship. Must be giving. Unselfish. Centered in another rather than in self. Willing to experience the bad news in his or her own life. Willing to be vulnerable, to be "public" with weakness, to know the joy of a friendship that won't be shattered when we are most ourselves—in weakness as well as strength.

Great friendships are pretty rare these days. Christians are the best hope for revival.

Evangelism
And how powerful are the implications for evangelism! "He who receives you receives me, and he who receives me receives him who sent me."

How many times have we been turned off by gimmicks

in evangelism? How many times have we felt we could never engage in the kind of personal evangelism offered in many churches? We often feel that we are not "specialists" in this field. We feel that because we are not enrolled on the personal evangelism team, we are not important to the task of evangelism. But, is that really true?

Not everyone can be skillful in every method that is advanced to win people to Jesus. But, does that mean you are unimportant? How could a person be like Jesus who felt no involvement in seeking people for Him? Obviously, he or she couldn't. Then what have we done? Haven't we interpreted evangelism too narrowly? Have we left the impression that evangelism is something to be done each Tuesday evening when a small group goes out to teach? Have we not greatly limited the power of our fellowship to reach out to others?

You see, the critical aspect of evangelism is whether you will be received by others. This means, as we have pointed out, that you must be willing to receive them as God is willing to receive them. It also says something about your being received. This means that you must never be unaware of who you are or the importance attached to *every* relationship. It means we carry the most important ingredient of evangelism in our persons. Therefore, we move about in our offices with a new vision of what it means to relate to the people in the office. We go to school with a new sense of significance for every person we know. It is true in the factory, in the home, when we shop—wherever we are. No meeting with a person is insignificant. We are now aware that what another person feels during that meeting can deeply affect his or her acceptance of Christ. I must, then, be the kind of person that recommends my Lord. My life must bear His image. My attitude must not hinder the possibility of His entrance into another life. I cannot cling to personality quirks but rather submit them to His Lordship.

What growth potential lies here! For me personally as well as for the kingdom.

I go out in search of persons who will receive me. This is evangelism. I'm not simply trying to find someone with whom I can have a Bible study. Rather, I'm trying to be the person God wants me to be, to relate to others in the way God relates to them in hopes that they will receive me and in receiving me open the way for Christ to enter their lives.

No manipulation here. No tricks are needed. Just genuine disciples. Nothing is more powerful than the life of a disciple. Life spreads life.

So, wherever you go, this is your mission. It works in any situation. You are special. You are needed. You are God's gift to others.

"He who receives you receives me, and he who receives me receives him who sent me."